LEADER
GUIDE

OVER ONE MILLION TRAINED

TRAINING *for* SERVICE

A BASIC BIBLE OVERVIEW

FOR EVERY CHRISTIAN

26-SESSION CERTIFICATION PROGRAM

Standard®
PUBLISHING

Cincinnati, Ohio

CONTENTS

HOW TO USE THIS BOOK 3

LESSON PLANS FOR LESSONS 1–26 4

REPRODUCIBLE WORKSHEETS 30

EXAM 1 (LESSONS 1–13) 40

EXAM 2 (LESSONS 14–26) 42

FINAL EXAM 44

ANSWERS FOR EXAMS 47

REPRODUCIBLE CERTIFICATE 48

THE ENTIRE TEXT OF THE *TRAINING FOR SERVICE STUDENT GUIDE* FOLLOWS.

Published by Standard Publishing, Cincinnati, Ohio
www.standardpub.com

Copyright © 1907, 1934, 1942, 1964, 1983, 1998, 2011 by Standard Publishing

Also available: *Training for Service Student Guide*, ISBN 978-0-7847-3301-1, copyright © 2011 by Standard Publishing

Printed in: United States of America
Authors: Jim Eichenberger, 2011; Eleanor Daniel, 1983; Orrin Root, 1964; Cecil James (C. J.) Sharp, 1934; Herbert Moninger, 1907
Project editor: Lynn Lusby Pratt
Cover design: Faceout Studio
Interior design: Dina Sorn at Ahaa! Design

All Scripture quotations—as well as the spellings of names, places, and scriptural terms—are taken from the *King James Version* of the Bible.

ISBN 978-0-7847-3300-4

17 16 15 14 13 12   2 3 4 5 6 7 8 9 10

HOW TO USE THIS BOOK

For over a century, *Training for Service* has equipped more than 1 million volunteers with this basic course and certification for Bible teaching. Ideal for those planning to teach Sunday school, serve as church leaders, or facilitate small groups, it is also recommended for anyone who just wants a Bible 101 course.

As a certification course

The original intent of this course was to give volunteer teachers and church leaders a baseline of biblical knowledge so they could undertake their tasks with confidence. While *Training for Service* also works well as a basic Bible literacy class for Sunday schools or small groups, many still use the course for its original purpose in this way:

1. Offer the course at various times throughout the year to accommodate busy schedules.

2. Decide which volunteers should be certified, systematically enroll them, keep track of those who successfully complete the course, and make plans to certify future volunteers.

3. Make arrangements for individual instruction. A certification class requires that those being certified meet a set standard. For that reason, you will need to give thought as to how you will arrange for content to be made up when a session needs to be missed, and how and when to retest a class member who did not pass the final certification exam. You may also wish to make arrangements for offering this class as a supervised self-study.

Contents of this book

In addition to the entire text of the *Training for Service Student Guide,* you will find these:

1. A suggested **lesson plan** is included for each session. The lesson plans assume that each student has his or her own book and has prepared for class in advance.

2. **Reproducible worksheets** are included for many sessions.

3. Give **exams** after the first 13 and after the final 13 sessions. Then the final exam must be passed with a score of 70 percent or higher in order for the student to be certified.

4. A reproducible **certificate of course completion** is found on page 48 of this book.

Additional materials

The reproducible worksheets, exams, and completion certificate may be downloaded from www.trainingforservice.com.

The following materials from Standard Publishing, in addition to the resources described on page 7 of the *Student Guide,* can enhance your *Training for Service* experience:

1. *Discovering God's Story* (ISBN 978-0-7847-2398-2) is a presentation of 100 key events, succinctly summarized and beautifully illustrated. *Discovering God's Story* reveals how individual Bible stories fit together as 1 continuous saga.

2. The Standard Reference Library provides a thorough yet concise look at the entire Bible:
- Old Testament Volume 1: *The Pentateuch* (ISBN 978-0-7847-1904-6)
- Old Testament Volume 2: *The History of Israel* (ISBN 978-0-7847-1905-3)
- Old Testament Volume 3: *Poetry and Prophecy* (ISBN 978-0-7847-1906-0)
- New Testament Volume 1: *The Life and Ministry of Jesus* (ISBN 978-0-7847-1900-8)
- New Testament Volume 2: *The New Testament Church* (ISBN 978-0-7847-1901-5)

HOW WE GOT OUR BIBLE

ATTENTION

Arrange to have a display of various Bible versions for the students to examine as they arrive. Include at least a Greek New Testament, *King James Version, American Standard Version, Revised Standard Version, Today's English Version, New American Standard Bible, New International Version, New King James Version,* and *New Living Translation.* Other old versions would be interesting, if they are available. Be sure to label each Bible, using its correct title. Place a sheet of paper with these instructions nearby: "Look up a familiar verse or passage such as John 3:16 in each version (except the Greek New Testament, unless you know Greek). Read the passage and compare the wording from version to version. Do different wordings alter the basic message?" Allot 5–7 minutes past the beginning time for this activity.

Introduce the Bible survey course upon which the class is embarking. Explain that the basis for today's lesson will be the following questions: 1) How did we get our Bible? 2) How did it begin? 3) How has it been handed down to us?

DISCOVERY

Form groups of 3. Assign each group the following Scriptures: 1 Corinthians 2:13; 1 Thessalonians 2:13; 2 Timothy 3:16; 2 Peter 1:20, 21; and Revelation 22:18, 19. Instruct each group to read the verses and find the answer to this question: "What does the Bible say about its authorship and purpose?" Allow 5 minutes for this; then discuss their findings. Emphasize that all Scripture—every bit—is God-breathed.

Assign small groups (or the larger group) to discuss *inspiration* and determine a definition. After the discussion, share this definition: "*Inspiration* is God's revelation communicated to us through writers who used their own minds and words, yet God so directed their lives and thoughts that the words they used in writing were the very words of God." Emphasize that 40 writers wrote the Bible over a period of 1,500 years.

Give a brief lecture of the material "Ancient Manuscripts and Versions."

Let the students share their findings from the "Attention" step.

Allow time for questions.

CLOSING

Summarize today's session.

Lead a time of prayer in which you give thanks to God for inspired revelation that has been preserved through the centuries so we can enjoy the Bible even today.

ASSIGNMENT

Remind the students that the key to the success of this class is for each person to come to class prepared. Encourage them to answer the end-of-chapter questions during the week.

Assign 2 students to prepare 5-minute presentations on the 2 ways we know about God. One will address natural revelation and the other, special revelation.

GOD'S WORD TO US

ATTENTION

Write this statement on the board: "Ultimately the question of the authority of Scriptures is a matter of faith and not of argument" (Martin Lloyd-Jones). Group the class members by 3s and ask them to decide whether they agree or disagree with the statement and why. Give each group a sheet of paper and a marker to record their answers and reasons. Allow 5 or 6 minutes for making these lists and sharing them with the entire class.

DISCOVERY

Begin this section of the lesson by inviting the individuals assigned to present their short reports. Be prepared to mention any material from the *Student Guide* that was omitted.

Then ask the students to turn to Philemon in their Bibles. Explain that the class will do a study using the principles mentioned. Distribute copies of the Lesson 2 Worksheet from page 30 or from www.trainingforservice.com. (To be ready to help students, you should have worked through the process yourself.) Allow 15 minutes for class members to work in small groups to read the book (per question 1) and answer questions 2, 9, and 2 others as assigned. Let the groups report.

Emphasize how important it is to determine the Bible's trustworthiness if we are to apply its principles today. Then discuss the following questions:

1. Why must we regard the Bible as authoritative if we are to gain the most from its study?

2. How does reading the total context help you in your study?

3. How do the principles of study discussed today help you?

CLOSING

Summarize the day's session. Encourage the students to begin to incorporate these Bible study principles into their Bible study this week. Close with prayer.

ASSIGNMENT

Encourage each student to read lesson 3 before the next class session.

Ask for volunteers to read 1 book from each section of the Bible. Each volunteer should read a different book. Suggested books from the Old Testament are Genesis, Ruth, Ecclesiastes, and Micah. Suggested books from the New Testament are Mark, Acts, 1 John, and Revelation. Ask each to come with a brief summary of the content of the book he or she read.

Encourage all class members to begin reading the Old Testament this week.

DIVISIONS OF THE BIBLE

ATTENTION

As class members arrive, distribute copies of the Lesson 3 Worksheet from page 30 or from www.trainingforservice.com. Allot 5 minutes for this activity. Go over the correct answers. (Questions 1, 2, 5, 8, and 10 refer to the Old Testament; all others refer to the New.)

Remind the class that today's lesson is an overview of the composition of the Bible.

DISCOVERY

Draw an open Bible on the board. Point out that this book, the Bible, is composed of 66 books grouped into 2 major divisions, the Old Testament and the New Testament. Each division is further subdivided into 4 parts.

Outline the 4 divisions of the Old Testament on the left side of the Bible drawing. Include the number of books in each. Ask the person who read a book from each section to give a 1- or 2-sentence summary of the types of literature included in that section. Add interesting facts from the *Student Guide* material. When you have completed the overview, have class members recite together the names of the divisions and numbers of books. Repeat the same procedure for the New Testament divisions.

Now play a game to make sure the students have the information firmly in mind. Draw 8 squares on the board as shown below. Explain that these represent the 4 groups of books in the Old Testament and in the New Testament. Ask students to name the groups in unison as you point to each square.

□□□□   □□□□

Divide the class into 2 teams. You will name a player whose turn it is to play. Point to a square and ask either "What kind?" or "How many?" When you ask "What kind?" the player is to name the division of the Bible. When you ask "How many?" the player gives the number of books in the group. A correct answer must be given within 10 seconds and will count as 1 point for the team. Make sure each player gets at least 1 turn.

Then continue by having the student give a fact about the division selected. Any correct information is acceptable except for "what kind" and "how many." A fact once used cannot be repeated. Follow the same time and scoring guidelines as before. Continue playing until you have no more time or until no more information can be supplied about any division.

CLOSING

Summarize the lesson for today. Review the divisions of the Bible again. Then read Romans 12 as an example of the letters written to guide Christian living. Close in prayer.

ASSIGNMENT

Ask class members to read lesson 4 for next time. Encourage them to begin to memorize the names of the books of the Old Testament.

Ask them to read 1 book of the Old Testament during the week. You may want to assign different books so students can assist in the presentation next time.

BOOKS OF THE OLD TESTAMENT

ATTENTION

As class members arrive, distribute copies of the Lesson 4 Worksheet from page 33 or from www.trainingforservice.com. Ask each to see how many names of the Old Testament books he or she can find. This will reinforce familiarity with the names of the books of the Old Testament. Allot 10 minutes for this activity. You may wish to distribute copies of your completed puzzle for students to check their answers.

Make the transition into the next section by pointing out that today's lesson deals with the books of the Old Testament and the basic content of each.

DISCOVERY

Quickly review the names of the 4 sections of the Old Testament.

Begin with the books of Law. Call on various class members to supply the names of the books in order. As they do, you or a student should write the abbreviations of the names on the board. Ask class members to summarize the contents of each book as you go. (Those who read a particular book during the week could do this.) Add any information not covered by the students. Do the same with the books of History, Poetry, and Prophecy. Be careful to pace yourself so that all the Old Testament can be covered during the session.

Go over the list of book names several times, section by section, repeating the books in unison. Then go around the class, with each student naming a book. Time this and see if the time can be shortened when the process is repeated.

CLOSING

You may want to prepare a handout sheet for your class that lists the books of the Old Testament and summarizes the contents. (Check the resources listed on page 3, as well as those on page 7 of the *Student Guide*.) If you do this, hand it out now instead of earlier in order to maintain individual attention to class activity.

Briefly summarize the lesson for today. Then close with prayer.

ASSIGNMENT

Encourage students to complete the task of memorizing the names of the books of the Old Testament.

Ask the class members to read lesson 5 for next time. Encourage them to begin work to master the names of the New Testament books.

Ask the class members to read 1 book of the New Testament during the coming week. As you did last session, you may want to assign each person to read a different book so each can have something to contribute during the presentation. Instruct each person to be prepared with a 1- or 2-sentence summary of the book's contents.

BOOKS OF THE NEW TESTAMENT

ATTENTION

As the class members arrive, distribute copies of the Lesson 5 Worksheet from page 31 or from www.trainingforservice.com. You may wish to distribute copies of your completed puzzle to allow students to check their answers. (**Across:** 3. Luke; 4. Titus; 9. Philippians; 10. Colossians; 11. Hebrews; 13. Corinthians; 15. Timothy. **Down:** 1. Thessalonians; 2. Jude; 5. John; 6. Galatians; 7. Mark; 8. James; 12. Romans; 14. Philemon)

DISCOVERY

Review the 4 sections of the New Testament. Begin with the Gospels. Call on class members to supply the names. As they do, you or a student can write abbreviations of the names on the board, as you did with the Old Testament books. Ask those who read a book to summarize the content of those books as you go. Add any pertinent information. Do the same with the books of History, Letters, and Prophecy.

Go over the names of the New Testament books in unison once or twice. Also review the sections and names of the Old Testament books.

CLOSING

If you distributed an Old Testament summary sheet last time, you will want to do the same for the New Testament books.

Briefly summarize today's lesson. Close with prayer.

ASSIGNMENT

Ask the class members to read lesson 6 before the next session. Encourage them to continue reading through the Bible and to work on memorizing the names of the books of the Bible.

Select 3 students to prepare presentations for the 3 dispensations of Bible history. They should use the *Student Guide* material, but you may also refer them to the resources listed on page page 7 of the *Student Guide,* as well as any resources you have available from those listed on page 3 of the *Leader Guide.* They will have 5 minutes each for their presentations.

3 DISPENSATIONS

ATTENTION

As the class members arrive, give each person a copy of the exercise below or write it on the board. Ask students to form groups of 3. Allow 10 minutes for response and small group discussion. Then take a few minutes for the entire group to have a discussion centered on the responses.

AGREE OR DISAGREE

Decide whether you agree or disagree with each statement below. Be prepared to explain/ defend your answer to your small group.

1. Since worship has occurred in different ways throughout history with God's blessing, God will probably change it again. Agree/Disagree

2. The Old Testament isn't very important to a Christian. Agree /Disagree

3. God's way of dealing with people will probably change in the future. Agree/Disagree

© 2011 Standard Publishing. Permission is granted to reproduce this page for ministry purposes only—not for resale.

DISCOVERY

Begin with a game to review the sections and names of the Bible books. Divide into 2 groups. The first person in the first group must name the first section of the Old Testament. The first person in the other group names the first book of the first section. Go back and forth from team to team, first naming all Law books, then identifying the second section and its books. Continue with the third and fourth sections. Follow the same pattern for the New Testament. (If a person answers incorrectly, go to the other team.) Each correct answer is worth 1 point. Spend no more than 10 minutes on this game.

Read Hebrews 1:1, 2 to introduce the idea of dispensations. Let the 3 speakers (assigned last time) present their reports. Time them so that no speaker exceeds 5 minutes. After the speakers have finished, add any omitted details. Then review the time line found on page 31 of the *Student Guide*. Point out how all the information fits together.

CLOSING

Summarize the material for the day. Use any extra time to review the names of the books of the Bible and the 3 dispensations. Close with prayer.

ASSIGNMENT

Ask the class members to read lesson 7 prior to the next class session. Ask them to become familiar with each place mentioned and to find it on a Bible map, because they will be asked to do so in class next time. Encourage them to practice by drawing a map and locating the places mentioned in the lesson. You may want to recommend the *Standard Bible Atlas,* in addition to the map on page 33 of the *Student Guide,* to assist the students in their study. Explain that if they have the map well enough in mind to draw it from memory, they can easily place Old Testament people and events in their geographical contexts.

Also encourage them to continue reading through the Bible.

THE OLD TESTAMENT WORLD

ATTENTION

As the class members arrive, distribute copies of the Lesson 7 Worksheet from page 33 or from www.trainingforservice.com. Ask them to work on it until you are ready to proceed. Go over the answers together. (1. D; 2. B; 3. C; 4. B; 5. C; 6. A; 7. A; 8. B; 9. B; 10. C; 11. D; 12. D; 13. B; 14. C; 15. D)

Point out that these are the places of the Old Testament world that form the basis of today's lesson.

DISCOVERY

Give each person a copy of the blank map you made from the map on page 32 (also available at www.trainingforservice.com). Ask everyone to fill in their maps as you present the material today. Refer to the complete map on page 33 of the *Student Guide* or use a large map of the Old Testament world, if available.

Point out the east end of the Mediterranean (called the great sea in the Old Testament) with the Nile River flowing into it from Egypt. To the southeast is the 2-horned end of the Red Sea. To the northeast is the head of the Euphrates River that flows through Mesopotamia to the Persian Gulf. Near the Euphrates is the Tigris River. Be sure to identify every place mentioned in today's lesson in the *Student Guide* (land areas, bodies of water, mountains), as well as historical highlights.

CLOSING

Summarize today's material. Use any extra time to review material from previous lessons.

ASSIGNMENT

Ask the students to read lesson 8 before the next session. Ask 8 volunteers to prepare a 3-minute report each on 1 of the 8 major characters in the lesson. Reports might include these features:

- the person's identity and main events of his life
- the person's strengths and weaknesses
- people associated with his life
- how God used this person in His plan

OLD TESTAMENT PEOPLE —PART 1

ATTENTION

Before the students begin to arrive, write the following statement on the board: "A Christian should study the Old Testament because . . ."

Ask each person to discuss with 2 other people how they each might complete the sentence. Then lead a general discussion to develop a list of reasons for studying the Old Testament. Write those on the board. (You could close the exercise by referring the class to the chart on page 60 of the *Student Guide.*)

Lead into today's lesson with a brief review of the previous 5 lessons. Point out that today's lesson deals with 8 of the 16 major characters of the Old Testament.

DISCOVERY

Proceed with the 8 presentations assigned in the last session. Time each so that no speaker exceeds 3 minutes.

CLOSING

Use any extra time to play a game. As you refer to the chart on page 37 in the *Student Guide,* ask the first player to name the first major character, the next a lesser character, the next a place, and the next an event. Do this for all 8 major characters. Each person who gives a correct answer receives 1 point.

ASSIGNMENT

Ask the students to read lesson 9 before the next class.

Get 8 more volunteers (preferably different from today's) to make 3-minute reports on the final 8 major Old Testament characters.

Encourage all students to continue memorizing Bible sections and books, dispensations, and characters.

OLD TESTAMENT PEOPLE —PART 2

ATTENTION

As the class members arrive, distribute copies of the Lesson 9 Worksheet from page 34 or from www.trainingforservice.com. You may wish to distribute copies of your completed puzzle to allow students to check their answers. (Adam, Noah, Abraham, Joseph, Moses, Joshua, Gideon, Samuel, Saul, David, Solomon, Elijah, Isaiah, Jeremiah, Daniel, Nehemiah; leading men)

DISCOVERY

Move into the 8 biographical presentations assigned last time. Be sure that no presentation exceeds 3 minutes.

CLOSING

Use any extra time to play the game suggested for the last session, using the second chart of 8 characters on page 40 of the *Student Guide* as your key.

ASSIGNMENT

Ask the students to study lesson 10 for the next class session. Encourage them to read (or at least skim) each Scripture passage listed in the *Student Guide*. Also ask them to memorize the periods of Old Testament history mentioned at the beginning of the lesson.

Get 6 volunteers to prepare 4-minute reports on the 6 events covered in lesson 10.

OLD TESTAMENT PERIODS —PART 1

ATTENTION

As the class members arrive, distribute copies of the Lesson 10 Worksheet from page 35 or from www.trainingforservice.com. Allow up to 10 minutes for the students to complete this. Then go over the answers together. (Obadiah, letters, decline, Tigris, Ezra, Solomon, Timothy, Assyria, Mesopotamia, Esther, Nehemiah, Thessalonians, probation, Egypt, redemption, Isaiah, Old Testament, Daniel, servitude)

DISCOVERY

Turn with the group to the chart on page 47 of the *Student Guide*. Have them follow the content from the first 2 periods as the reports are presented by the 6 people assigned. Be sure that reports are limited to 4 minutes each.

Divide the class into 6 small groups. Assign 1 event from today's lesson to each group. Ask each to develop a 1-minute sermon to answer: "What does this event of history teach us?" Allot 5 minutes for them to prepare, then 1 minute each for the presentations.

CLOSING

Use any extra time to review the information in lessons 3–9. Use the *Student Guide* questions from those lessons to assist you. Close with prayer.

ASSIGNMENT

Ask the students to read lesson 11 before the next class session. Encourage them to continue reading the Old Testament by reading at least 1 more book this week.

Find more volunteers to prepare 4-minute reports on the 7 events covered in lesson 11.

Encourage class members to review the material covered during the course in order to fix facts in their memories.

OLD TESTAMENT PERIODS —PART 2

ATTENTION

Divide the board in half with a vertical line. As the students enter, draw their attention to this sentence, which you have written on the left side of the board: "Bible study is important for me because . . ." Ask each person to think of 2 or 3 ways to complete the sentence and to share their responses with a group of 3 other people. Allow the groups 5 minutes for discussion before leading a general discussion. List the most common/popular responses on the left side of the board.

Continue the discussion by asking: "Why is this course of study important? What have you gained from it so far?" List these answers on the right side of the board.

Then make the transition into today's material by pointing out that 2 more periods of Bible history will be studied.

DISCOVERY

Turn with the group to the chart on page 47 of the *Student Guide.* Have them follow the content from the third and fourth periods as your volunteers present their 4-minute reports. (Note additional information about kings and prophets on the chart on page 50 of the *Student Guide.*)

Divide the class into small groups, dividing the 7 events from these 2 periods among them. Ask each group to decide what major lesson is to be learned from each event. Instruct them to put that lesson to music, using the tune of a commonly known commercial jingle. State that they will sing to the rest of the class in order to encourage everyone to heed this lesson. Allow up to 10 minutes for them to decide on the lesson and to compose the jingle. Then have each group share its jingle, singing it for the entire group. Take a few minutes to emphasize the importance of heeding these lessons.

CLOSING

Prepare a pep talk to conclude this session. Emphasize the value of Bible study and the importance of having a firm grasp of background details as an aid to understanding the biblical text. Praise the students who have prepared faithfully during the course of these first 11 sessions. Encourage them to continue their careful preparation. Urge others to follow their example. Close with prayer.

ASSIGNMENT

Ask class members to read and prepare lesson 12 prior to the next session. Encourage them to review lessons 1–11 so they can identify the books of the Bible as well as major geographical areas and sites, major characters, and the periods of Old Testament history.

Get 2 volunteers to prepare 6-minute reports: 1 on the period of decline and the other on the first 2 parts of the period of servitude in lesson 12.

Encourage all class members to continue reading the Old Testament books. Urge them especially to read the Bible accounts of each event in the lesson.

OLD TESTAMENT PERIODS —PART 3

ATTENTION

As the class members arrive, distribute copies of the Lesson 12 Worksheet from page 34 or from www.trainingforservice.com. Allow up to 10 minutes for the students to complete this. Then go over the answers together. (1. D; 2. E; 3. F; 4. C; 5. B; 6. F; 7. A; 8. B; 9. B; 10. D; 11. A; 12. F; 13. D; 14. F; 15. E; 16. A; 17. C; 18. C)

DISCOVERY

Turn with the group to the chart on page 47 of the *Student Guide.* Have them follow the content from the final 2 periods as your volunteers (assigned last time) present their reports. Be sure that reports are limited to 6 minutes. Then you can present a brief lecture on parts 2–7 of the period of servitude (*Student Guide* p. 46), also using information from "Between the Testaments" (*Student Guide* p. 48).

CLOSING

Lead a brief discussion centered on this topic: "What lessons can we learn from each of the 6 Old Testament periods?" Close with prayer.

ASSIGNMENT

Ask the students to read lesson 13 before the next session. Encourage the students to continue reading the Old Testament.

Ask a volunteer to prepare a report on the altar and the sacrificial system. Encourage that person to read Leviticus to find a description of the various sacrifices. Another volunteer may make a special study of the tabernacle and be prepared to discuss the importance of each part.

ALTAR AND TABERNACLE

ATTENTION

As the students arrive, have them form groups of 3. Provide pens and paper. Then ask the groups to prepare an acrostic that helps define the word *worship*. Here are 2 samples:

We **O**ffer **R**everence and **S**ervice to **H**eaven **I**n **P**raise.

Wonderful God, **O**ur hearts **R**each up, **S**eeking **H**elp and **I**nviting your **P**resence.

After 5 minutes, invite class members to share their responses as you write them on the board. Then make the transition into the lesson theme for the day.

DISCOVERY

Let the reporter who studied the sacrificial system and the altar present his or her findings. Be prepared to fill in the details, if necessary. Be sure that the students understand the purpose of the sacrificial system.

Then ask the class to turn to the illustration of the tabernacle on page 53 of the *Student Guide* to refer to the illustration as the volunteer who studied the tabernacle system presents that report. Add any important details not covered by the report. Be sure that the students understand the symbolism for each part of the tabernacle.

Follow through by having class members identify a part or piece of furniture in the tabernacle and tell about size, materials, use, and symbolism. Weather permitting, you may wish to have your group use sidewalk chalk to map out the dimensions of the tabernacle and its furnishings on the church parking lot!

Lead a discussion answering these questions: 1) Why did God give so much attention to the worship system in the Old Testament? 2) What lessons can we learn from this?

Point out that the book of Hebrews in the New Testament reviews the Old Testament system, then presents Jesus as superior to that system.

CLOSING

Reemphasize that worship is a privilege never to be taken for granted. Stress that God has always provided a means for people to fellowship with Him. Close with prayer.

ASSIGNMENT

Encourage the students to review lessons 1–13 in preparation for the exam over the first half of this study. Arrange a time to give the exam.

Ask the class members to study lesson 14 before the next class session. Ask a volunteer to prepare a report about the temple and another volunteer to prepare a presentation about the synagogue.

Encourage class members to read the book of Hebrews this week.

TEMPLE AND SYNAGOGUE

ATTENTION

As class members arrive, write the following words on the board: *church, cathedral, temple, chapel, shrine, sanctuary,* and *synagogue.* Ask group members to informally gather in small groups to discuss how these words are similar to each other and how they differ. Allow 2–3 minutes for this activity. When all members have arrived, have volunteers share their ideas about those words.

Tell them that while all the words may refer to places of worship, you will study 2 that have very special significance in Old Testament worship.

DISCOVERY

Have the person who prepared the report on the temple present it at this time.

Assign each of the following Scriptures to a pair of students. Ask each pair to read the Scripture and identify the part(s) of the temple where each event occurred. Allow 3–5 minutes. Be available to answer questions and offer suggestions.

1. Luke 1:5-23. Zechariah was burning incense in the holy place.
2. Luke 2:21-39. It is likely that Simeon and Anna greeted Jesus in the court of women. But Joseph would have taken the doves into the court of Israel, and the priests would have sacrificed them at the altar in the court of priests.
3. John 2:13-17. The market was in the court of Gentiles.
4. John 10:22, 23. Solomon's porch was on the east side of the court of Gentiles.
5. Mark 12:41-44. The treasury was in the court of women.
6. Acts 21:17-39. Paul was probably seized in the court of women and dragged out into the court of Gentiles.

Ask for the presentation of the report on the synagogue by the person who prepared it. Be prepared yourself so you can fill in any details.

Now develop a brief discussion around the following: 1) Compare and contrast the temple and the tabernacle. 2) Compare and contrast the temple, a synagogue, and a church building. 3) What lessons can we learn from God's careful provision for Old Testament worship?

CLOSING

Remind the students of how very important worship has been and is to God, both in the Old Testament era and now. Close with a prayer of praise.

ASSIGNMENT

Ask the class members to prepare lesson 15 before class time. Encourage them to continue their reading in the Old Testament.

Assign each of 6 volunteers 1 of the 6 feasts of the Israelites. Ask each volunteer to prepare a 3-minute report. Encourage them to use a Bible dictionary to assist in preparation.

THE JEWISH FEASTS

ATTENTION

As the students arrive, ask them to notice the following sentences, which you have written on the board: 1) When I worship God, I . . . 2) When I think of a feast, I think of . . . 3) When I want to remember something significant, I . . .

Give them 4–6 minutes to think of ways they might complete those and to share their responses with 3 neighbors. Then ask the entire group: "What do those 3 statements have in common?" Develop the discussion around the idea that feasts were times of remembrance and worship in the Old Testament. We sometimes lose that significance in this era.

DISCOVERY

Now let the students who prepared reports about each of the feasts present their findings. Fill in any essential details that were left unmentioned.

Show how the feasts mentioned in John's Gospel help to date the ministry of Jesus. Ask volunteers to read the following passages:

1. John 2:13-16. It was Passover when Jesus drove the merchants out of the temple.

2. John 5:1-9. This was probably the Passover, for John 4:35 identifies it to be 4 months until harvest, and the other feasts had passed.

3. John 6:1-11. This was Passover time.

4. John 13:1-17. Jesus ate the last supper at Passover.

Since 4 Passovers are mentioned, we conclude that Jesus' ministry extended more than 3 years.

Give a brief lecture on the Day of Atonement. Show how it differed from the 6 feasts. Point out its significance and procedure.

Feasts in Old Testament times had religious significance. Each feast commemorated a special event in Israel's history. What can we learn from this for our day?

CLOSING

Summarize the content of the last 3 lessons. If you have time, lead a quick review of the first 15 lessons, since this concludes the Old Testament survey. Close with prayer.

ASSIGNMENT

Ask the students to study lesson 16 prior to the next class session and to answer the *Student Guide* questions at the end of the chapter. Encourage them to familiarize themselves with the maps on pages 63 and 64 of the *Student Guide* and to continue their Bible reading, perhaps adding New Testament reading to their Old Testament meditation this week.

NEW TESTAMENT LANDS

ATTENTION

As the class members arrive, distribute copies of the Lesson 16 Worksheet from page 36 or from www.trainingforservice.com. Allow up to 10 minutes for the students to complete this. Then go over the answers together. (1. B; 2. E; 3. H; 4. A; 5. F; 6. D; 7. I; 8. G; 9. C; 10. J) Remind the students that all these places are mentioned often in the New Testament. Our task is to become thoroughly familiar with them.

DISCOVERY

Turn with your group to the maps on pages 63 and 64 in the *Student Guide.* Ask students to locate places on the maps as you talk about them. Give pertinent facts about the places in lesson 16: Mediterranean coast, Jordan River, Galilee, Samaria, Judea, Perea, Decapolis, the tetrarchy of Philip, Jerusalem, Bethlehem, Nazareth, and Capernaum. (Be sure you have prepared carefully, using a Bible dictionary, Bible atlas, and the New Testament as resource materials.)

Divide your class into 5 groups. Have the first group complete assignments 1–4 from the 8 options below. Assign the other 4 groups 1 each of options 5–8.

1. Locate the approximate site where a man was beaten by robbers in the parable found in Luke 10:30-37.

2. Find where Jesus fed the 5,000: John 6:1 and Luke 9:10.

3. Estimate the distance from Jerusalem to Bethany. How does that help you understand Matthew 21:17, 18? Estimate the distance from Nazareth to Jerusalem. How long would it take to walk that distance?

4. Locate the places mentioned in Acts 11:26; Acts 28:16; 1 Corinthians 1:2; and 2 Corinthians 1:1.

5. Trace Paul's first missionary tour, Acts 13, 14.

6. Trace Paul's second missionary tour, Acts 15:36–18:22.

7. Trace Paul's third missionary tour, Acts 18:23–21:15.

8. Trace Paul's voyage to Rome, Acts 27:1–28:16.

CLOSING

Summarize the session and close with prayer.

ASSIGNMENT

Urge the students to read lesson 17 before the next session.

Ask them to devote some time to a review to make sure they have a grasp on the details of lessons 1–16.

Encourage them to continue reading the Bible in their times of meditation.

THE CHRIST IN PROPHECY

ATTENTION

Have this heading on the board for the students to consider as they enter the classroom: "Examples of predictions that did not come true." Ask them to write examples under the heading as they think of them. Examples may include everything from weather to politics to sports.

Make the transition into the Bible study section by emphasizing that only the Bible has 100 percent success in predicting future events.

DISCOVERY

The Old Testament foretold the events of Jesus' life with amazing precision. Turn with the class to the messianic prophecies discussed on page 66 of the *Student Guide*. Take some time to have students look them up and explain them. Also look at just a few references of those prophecies' fulfillment in the New Testament:

1. Hope in the garden (Genesis 3:15; Romans 16:20)
2. The ultimate king (Genesis 49:10; Revelation 5:5-10)
3. A priest like Melchizedek (Genesis 14:18-20; Psalm 110:4; Hebrews 7:1-10)
4. A prophet like Moses (Deuteronomy 18:18; Acts 3:22-26)
5. The peacemaker from Bethlehem (Micah 5:2-8; Matthew 2:1-12)
6. The Son of God (Psalm 2; Acts 13:33; Hebrews 1:5)
7. God with us (Isaiah 7:14; Matthew 1:23)
8. The healing servant (Isaiah 35:5, 6; Matthew 11:5)
9. The suffering servant (Isaiah 53; Acts 8:32-35)
10. The Son of man (Daniel 7:13, 14; Acts 7:56)

Ask the class members to divide into groups of 3 to 5. Distribute copies of the Lesson 17 Worksheet from page 36 or from www.trainingforservice.com. Allow up to 10 minutes for the students to complete this. Then go over the answers together. (1. B; 2. E; 3. H; 4. A; 5. F; 6. D; 7. I; 8. G; 9. C; 10. J) Identify what prophecy was made and how it was fulfilled.

CLOSING

Reemphasize the uniqueness and divine origin of Bible prophecy. Close with prayer.

ASSIGNMENT

Ask students to prepare lesson 18 before class.

Get 10 volunteers who will present the 10 events from the first 2 periods of Jesus' life. Ask that reports be confined to 3 minutes each.

LIFE OF CHRIST—PART 1

ATTENTION

As the class members arrive, distribute copies of the Lesson 18 Worksheet from page 37 or from www.trainingforservice.com. Allot 10 minutes for this activity. You may wish to distribute copies of your completed puzzle for students to check their answers. (1. birth; 2. temptation; 3. temple; 4. nobleman; 5. baptism; 6. return; 7. flight; 8. Nicodemus; 9. miracle; 10. woman)

DISCOVERY

Remind students that the memory work in this lesson and the 2 following lessons will be helpful in their Bible study as long as they live.

Mention the 3 periods of New Testament history from page 68 of the *Student Guide*. Then help the students memorize the 7 separate periods of the life of Christ by listing them on the board:

- Period of Preparation
- Period of Obscurity
- Period of Popularity
- Period of Opposition
- Period of Persecution
- Passion Week
- Resurrection Appearances

Go over these 7 periods several times. Erase them randomly, 1 at a time, as the class names all the periods. Then remind them that this lesson and the next 2 will present 5 events from each period of Jesus' life.

Ask the first 5 students to present their reports (assigned last time). On the board, write the event that the report is about before the student gives it. Be sure that no report exceeds 3 minutes. Follow with the other 5 reports. After all the reports are finished, go over the list of events once more.

CLOSING

Use any remaining time to review the content from today. Close with prayer.

ASSIGNMENT

Ask the class members to prepare lesson 19 before the next session.

Encourage them to continue their Bible reading and also to work on memorization of the facts covered in this lesson. Point out that it will be better to spend a few minutes on this every day, or several times a day, than to study for a long time in a single period.

LIFE OF CHRIST—PART 2

ATTENTION

To begin the session, display various types of personal ID. These may include a driver's license, birth certificate, voter registration card, employee ID card, etc. Begin a discussion by asking: 1) When might you be asked for ID? 2) What type of ID would be best to use for that purpose?

After 5 minutes of discussion, make the transition into today's Bible study.

DISCOVERY

Review the 10 events from the life of Jesus covered last time. Then divide the class into 10 groups to study the 10 events in today's lesson. Give each group a large sheet of paper and markers. Assign 1 of the following passages to each group. Ask group members to read the Bible account and draw a picture to depict it.

1. The calling of the fishermen (Matthew 4:18-22)
2. The Sermon on the Mount (Matthew 5–7)
3. The widow's son (Luke 7:11-17)
4. The lakeside parables (Matthew 13)
5. Jairus's daughter (Matthew 9:18-26)
6. Feeding the 5,000 (Matthew 14:13-21)
7. The Syrophoenician's daughter (Mark 7:24-30)
8. Peter's confession (Matthew 16:13-17)
9. The transfiguration (Matthew 17:1-8)
10. The Good Samaritan (Luke 10:29-37)

Allot 10–12 minutes for this. Then have each group display its picture and give a brief statement of the event.

CLOSING

If time allows, review the events of this lesson and lesson 18. Close with prayer.

ASSIGNMENT

Ask the class members to prepare lesson 20 before the next class session.

Urge the students to continue work on memorization of the materials covered so far.

Encourage them to continue their Bible reading.

LIFE OF CHRIST—PART 3

ATTENTION

As the class members arrive, distribute copies of the Lesson 20 Worksheet from page 37 or from www.trainingforservice.com. It will serve as a good review of the preceding 2 lessons. Allow up to 10 minutes for the students to complete this. Then go over the answers together. (1. G; 2. A; 3. A; 4. C; 5. F; 6. D; 7. B; 8. A; 9. D; 10. C; 11. C; 12. E; 13. E; 14. F; 15. B; 16. B; 17. D; 18. E; 19. F; 20. A; 21. D; 22. F; 23. F; 24. B; 25. E)

Remind the class that this session considers the last 3 periods of Jesus' life.

DISCOVERY

Distribute the following 15 events among your students. If there are more than 15 in your class, have them work in small groups. Ask each to write an abridged edition of the assigned section. Each account should be stated in 1 sentence of 15 words or less.

1. Raising of Lazarus (John 11:1-16)
2. 10 healed of leprosy (Luke 17:11-19)
3. Little children (Matthew 19:13-15)
4. Rich young ruler (Luke 18:18-27)
5. Zaccheus (Luke 19:1-10)
6. Mary's anointing (Matthew 26:6-13)
7. Triumphal entry (Matthew 21:1-11)
8. 10 virgins (Matthew 25:1-13)
9. The upper room (Matthew 26:17-29)
10. Crucifixion (Mark 14:53–15:39)
11. Appearance to 2 (Luke 24:13-35)
12. Appearance to 10 (Luke 24:33-49)
13. Appearance to 7 (John 21:1-14)
14. Appearance to 500 (1 Corinthians 15:6)
15. Appearance to 11 (Matthew 28:16-20)

Allot 8–10 minutes for the groups to complete this. Then have each group present its abridged edition of the event.

CLOSING

Note that we have now finished our study of the life of Christ. Close with prayer.

ASSIGNMENT

Ask the class members to prepare lesson 21 before the next session. Urge them to continue their work on memorization of the details from previous lessons and to begin to memorize Matthew 28:19, 20.

Find a volunteer to prepare a 5-minute report on the meaning of the word *apostle* and what an apostle's qualifications are.

Encourage students to continue their Bible reading.

THE APOSTLES AND THE GREAT COMMISSION

ATTENTION

As the class members arrive, distribute copies of the Lesson 21 Worksheet from page 38 or from www.trainingforservice.com. Allow up to 10 minutes for the students to complete this. You may wish to give the group copies of your completed puzzle to check their own.

Make the transition into the Bible lesson by stating that the apostles were the appointed successors of Jesus to see that the 1st-century church was established.

DISCOVERY

Write each of the following passages on an index card and distribute those among the class members: Luke 6:12-16; Mark 2:13-17; Mark 3:13-19; Matthew 10:2-4; John 1:40-42, 45-49; John 14:22; John 21:2; and Acts 1:15-26.

Have the verses read aloud. In each case, list the names identified on the board. (If students are using assorted Bible versions, there will be variations.) Refer to the apostles' names in the *Student Guide* on page 77. Briefly discuss reasons for the differences in names and give examples of how we know people today by various names.

Let the assigned volunteer present the report on apostles. Illustrate the qualifications with Acts 1:21, 22; John 14:26; John 16:13; and Matthew 10:1.

Read each of the 3 Great Commission references noted on page 78 in the *Student Guide*. Challenge the students to memorize Matthew 28:19, 20 before next time. Point out that there are 3 questions that can help them memorize:

1. Therefore, go and do what? (Make disciples.)
2. Make disciples by doing what? (Baptizing them.)
3. And doing what? (Teaching them.)

When they have learned the basic answers to the questions, they simply add the rest of the phrases as they answer the questions. If you have time, work through the process with the students. Emphasize the role of each Christian in carrying out the commission.

CLOSING

Review the material from the previous New Testament lessons. Close with prayer.

ASSIGNMENT

Ask students to prepare lesson 22 before the next class session.

Write each of the following 8 passages on an index card: Acts 2:1-11; Acts 2:12-41; Acts 2:44, 45 and 4:32-37; Acts 5:1-10; Acts 6:1-6; Acts 6:8–7:60; Acts 8:1-4; and Acts 9:1-20. Assign 8 volunteers to prepare 3-minute reports for next time. Suggest that they check with your church library or the children's department for pictures, charts, outlines, or maps they might use.

BEGINNINGS OF THE CHURCH

ATTENTION

Type the words of Acts 8:4 in a large font. Print out and make a copy for each 3 to 5 students. Cut apart each copy, word by word, and put each set of pieces into a separate envelope. Divide the class into groups of 3 to 5 and give each group an envelope of words. Ask them to arrange a sensible statement from the words. Allow no more than 5 or 6 minutes for this. Lead a brief discussion centered on the students' reactions to the statement.

DISCOVERY

Have the assigned reports presented now. Encourage reporters to use the map on page 64 of the *Student Guide* to point out where the event of their reports happened. Be sure to keep the time to 3 minutes each. Between reports, fill in any gaps in information.

Now return the class to the groups they were in earlier. Give each group 1, 2, or 3 of the incidents from Acts that were included in the reports of your presentation. Ask each group to reread the sections and to determine any principles for the church today to apply. After 10 minutes, list their suggested principles on the board. At least the following should be included:

1. The church should grow numerically.
2. Christians care for each other's physical needs.
3. Gross sin must not be tolerated within the church.
4. Organization is acceptable and needed when it helps the church to meet particular needs.
5. Every Christian should feel responsible for spreading the good news.
6. The gospel is for every person everywhere.
7. Missions are at the heart of the church's purpose for existing.
8. The church is to worship and teach to help people grow spiritually.

Lead a brief discussion about how your church rates on application of the principles and how improvement could be made. Give everyone an index card and ask them to write a memo stating what they will do to help their church carry out the principles.

CLOSING

Review the material covered from lesson 16 through today. Emphasize geography and the life of Christ. Then reemphasize the need for the church today to be as much as possible like the church of the 1st century in function, attitude, and dynamics. Close with prayer.

ASSIGNMENT

Ask the class to prepare lesson 23 before the next class session. Remind the members to work on reviewing in preparation for the exam over lessons 14–26 and the final exam.

Ask a volunteer to prepare a 5-minute talk on baptism and another volunteer to do the same for the Lord's Supper. Encourage them to use Bible study helps in their preparation.

NEW LIFE IN CHRIST

ATTENTION

Before students arrive, draw a vertical line to divide the board in half. Write this on the left half: "A Christian is . . ." Invite arriving class members to write a completion of the sentence on the left half.

After several people have arrived, form groups of 3 to 5. Ask them to discuss this question: "How am I different this year than I was at this time last year?" Allow 3–5 minutes for this. Then list the responses on the right half of the board.

Tie together these 2 activities by pointing out that the implication of the question about differences is that change is expected in our lives. And the suggestions for completing the "A Christian is . . ." statement surely indicate that being a Christian does require continual growth and change. Today's lesson examines some of the changes that occur.

DISCOVERY

Ask the students to turn to 2 Corinthians 5. Ask them to work in pairs, using nothing but their Bibles, to list ways we become new when we become Christians. Each item listed provides a potential area of growth in the new life. The final list could include these:

1. New hope (vv. 1-3)
2. New purpose (v. 5)
3. New source of power (v. 5)
4. New confidence (v. 6)
5. New sense of direction (v. 7)
6. New standard of approval (v. 9)
7. New motivation (vv. 14, 15)
8. New standard of judgment (v. 16)
9. New work (v. 20)
10. Totally new person (v. 17)

Allow 10 minutes for the groups to work; then call for the reports. Spend time discussing what belongs in the list and why.

Then proceed to the assigned 5-minute reports on baptism and the Lord's Supper.

Now divide the class into 4 groups. Assign each group a topic to discuss. Each will begin with: "How would our lives change if we were to apply all of today's principles fully?" Give 1 group "at home," another "at work," another "in the community," and another "at church." Allot 3–5 minutes for the groups to work. Then call for reports and develop a discussion based on the group responses.

CLOSING

Take a few minutes to review the New Testament covered thus far in this course.

ASSIGNMENT

Ask the class members to prepare lesson 24 before the next class session. Encourage continued review plus commitment to regular Bible reading.

Get 3 volunteers to prepare 8- to 10-minute reports, 1 for each of the 3 sections in the lesson.

LIFE OF PAUL—PART 1

ATTENTION

As the class members arrive, distribute copies of the Lesson 24 Worksheet from page 38 or from www.trainingforservice.com. Allow up to 10 minutes for the students to complete this. You may wish to give the group copies of your completed puzzle to check their own.

Then explain that Paul's early life forms the content for today's lesson.

DISCOVERY

Point out that today's lesson covers the first 3 of these 6 periods of the life of Paul:
- Saul the student
- Saul the persecutor
- Saul the convert
- Paul the missionary
- Paul the author
- Paul the martyr

Now have the 3 people who prepared presentations make their reports. Be sure to fill in any omitted details. Review the chart on page 84 of the *Student Guide.*

CLOSING

Use any extra time for review of the New Testament material from lesson 16 through today. Emphasize the 6 periods of Paul's life. Then quickly review the details of this lesson. Close with prayer.

ASSIGNMENT

Ask the class members to prepare lesson 25 before the next class session. Encourage them to read Acts 13–28, which discloses the details of Paul's missionary travels.

Get 4 volunteers to prepare 5- to 8-minute reports on the 3 missionary journeys of Paul, plus his trip to Rome. Encourage them to prepare carefully, using the Bible material as the major basis for the reports.

Remind the students to work on reviewing the lessons in this study so they will be prepared for the exam over lessons 14–26 and the final exam.

LIFE OF PAUL—PART 2

ATTENTION

As the students arrive, ask them to prepare an acrostic, using a word or phrase for each letter that spells *missionary*. Provide pens and paper. This sample acrostic could be written on the board:

My responsibility
International
Sent
Spread good news
Into all the world
Overseas
Nearby
At home
Redemption
Your responsibility

DISCOVERY

Review the names of the 6 periods of Paul's life. Explain that this lesson covers the final 3 periods of Paul's life.

Have the 4 reporters who prepared presentations regarding Paul's 3 missionary journeys plus his voyage to Rome give their reports at this time. Keep them within the assigned time limits.

Briefly present the material on Paul the martyr and the writings of Peter and John. Include information about Peter's books and John's books of the New Testament. Remind students that dates given are approximate. We can be sure of the facts given in the Bible, and the dates we have are near enough to give a general idea of the time involved.

CLOSING

Use any remaining time to review the material from the New Testament lessons studied so far. Then close with prayer.

ASSIGNMENT

Ask the class members to prepare lesson 26 prior to the next class session. Urge them to work on reviewing the entire series of lessons.

Also encourage them to continue their Bible reading.

THE BIBLE FOR THE WHOLE WORLD

ATTENTION

As the class members arrive, distribute copies of the Lesson 26 Worksheet from page 39 or from www.trainingforservice.com. Allow up to 10 minutes for the students to complete this. Then go over the answers together. (**People**—1. H; 2. B; 3. A; 4. F; 5. C; 6. I; 7. D; 8. E; 9. G; 10. J. **Places**—1. F; 2. E; 3. C; 4. I; 5. J; 6. A; 7. B; 8. D; 9. H; 10. G. **Books**—1. G; 2. B; 3. J; 4. A; 5. H; 6. E; 7. C; 8. I; 9. F; 10. D)

Explain that today's lesson, the last in this study, will examine the work the church has yet to do.

DISCOVERY

Display a world map or a globe. Point to the world and explain that the world is the basis for the work of the church. Bring some materials from the missionaries your congregation supports, and locate their work on the map or globe. Summarize how each mission correlates to the content of this lesson.

CLOSING

Use the remaining minutes to answer questions about and/or to review the material covered during these weeks of study. Close with prayer.

ASSIGNMENT

Encourage the students to review course content in preparation for the exam over lessons 14–26 and the final exam. Arrange a time to give the exams to the students.

Urge them to continue in their regular Bible reading program.

LESSON 2 WORKSHEET

STUDYING PHILEMON

1. Read the entire book of Philemon.

2. Who wrote the book of Philemon?

3. To whom was Philemon written?

4. Write the key words in the text.

5. Develop a brief outline of the book.

6. Write a 1-sentence summary for each section of the outline.

7. Summarize the problem addressed in the book.

8. What was the intended meaning of verses 17-21?

9. What principles does this book present for living today?

LESSON 3 WORKSHEET

OLD TESTAMENT OR NEW TESTAMENT?

Mark each of these descriptions as applying either to the Old Testament (O) or the New Testament (N).

_____ 1. Collection of 39 books

_____ 2. 5 books of Law

_____ 3. 4 Gospels

_____ 4. 1 book of Prophecy

_____ 5. 5 books of Poetry

_____ 6. 21 Letters

_____ 7. Collection of 27 books

_____ 8. 17 books of Prophecy

_____ 9. 1 book of History

_____ 10. 12 books of History

LESSON 5 WORKSHEET

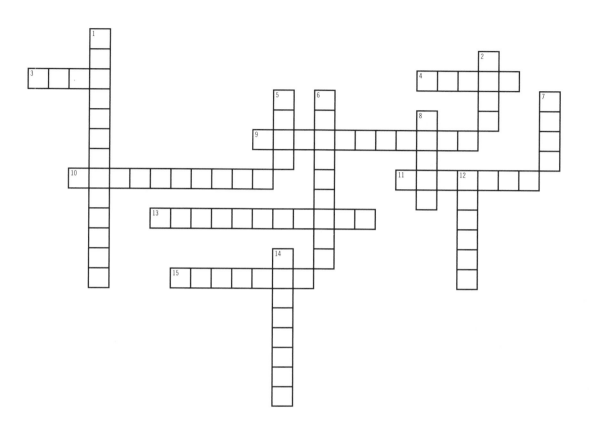

Across

3. Third Gospel
4. Paul's letter to an evangelist on Crete
9. Letter of joy
10. Letter after Philippians
11. Unsigned letter sometimes attributed to Paul
13. Paul wrote 2 letters to these Christians
15. Spiritual "son" of Paul

Down

1. Two letters of Paul dealing with Christian living and the second coming
2. Brother of James, son of Joseph
5. Beloved apostle and author of 4 books
6. Letter before Ephesians
7. Second Gospel
8. Practical letter found after Hebrews
12. Letter after Acts
14. Letter to a slave owner

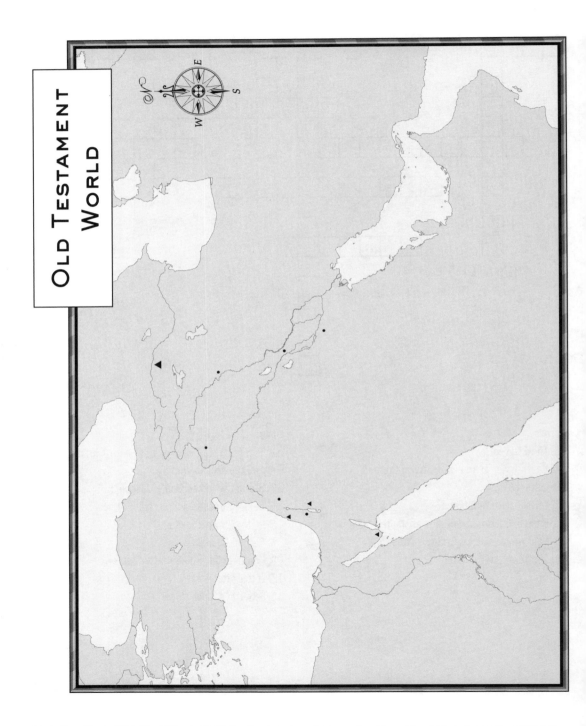

OLD TESTAMENT WORLD

LESSON 4 WORKSHEET

OLD TESTAMENT
BOOK SEARCH

Find the names of all the books of the Old Testament in the puzzle below—backward, forward, up, and down.

```
A D E C C L E S I A S T E S U W P
H A X T H U H A I M E H E N R L R
A N O V O H A G B N A H U M I K O
I I D B S J E J U D G E S S A V
D E U T E R O N O M Y E Z R A S E
A L S O A M N E B U H A C I M S R
B J O S H U A S A C H R O N U E B
O H A B B A H I M R E H T S E L S
E L P S A L M S O Z O J O E L C K
L E V I T I C U S O X W Y R L I U
K I O S N O G U S R E B M U N N K
I K N A Z E C H A R I A H T W O K
N E L I H A I N A H P E Z H O R A
G Z L A M E N T A T I O N S O H B
S E O H A G G A I Y Z N O T S C A
H A I M E R E J M A L A C H I A H
E G C N O M O L O S F O G N O S B
```

LESSON 7 WORKSHEET

MATCH THEM

Match each place below with its proper identification.

_____ 1. Tigris

_____ 2. Egypt

_____ 3. Ararat

_____ 4. Babylonia

_____ 5. Nebo

_____ 6. Red Sea

_____ 7. Mediterranean Sea

_____ 8. Assyria

_____ 9. Israel

_____ 10. Sinai

_____ 11. Euphrates

_____ 12. Nile

_____ 13. Persia

_____ 14. Carmel

_____ 15. Jordan

A. Body of water

B. Empire

C. Mountain

D. River

LESSON 9 WORKSHEET

OLD TESTAMENT CHARACTERS

Unscramble the names of the 16 main Old Testament characters below. Then unscramble the circled letters to find the surprise answer that fills in the squares.

DAMA _ _ _ _

NAHO _ _ _ _

BAHRAMA _ _ _ _ _ _ _

PHJESO _ _ _ _ _ _

SESMO _ _ _ _ _

SUHJAO _ _ _ _ _ _

GIDNOE _ _ _ _ _ _

LUSMEA _ _ _ _ _ _

AULS _ _ _ _

DADVI _ _ _ _ _

MOLOOSN _ _ _ _ _ _ _

JALHEI _ _ _ _ _ _

HAISIA _ _ _ _ _ _

JERIHMEA _ _ _ _ _ _ _ _

DENIAL _ _ _ _ _ _

HEANEHIM _ _ _ _ _ _ _ _

Like a Hollywood blockbuster, the Old Testament has an impressive cast of

☐☐☐☐☐☐ ☐☐☐ ☐☐☐ .

LESSON 12 WORKSHEET

PEOPLE BY PERIOD

Match the person with the period of Old Testament history in which he lived.

_____ 1. Abraham

_____ 2. Adam

_____ 3. Daniel

_____ 4. David

_____ 5. Elijah

_____ 6. Ezra

_____ 7. Gideon

_____ 8. Isaiah

_____ 9. Jeremiah

_____ 10. Joseph

_____ 11. Joshua

_____ 12. Malachi

_____ 13. Moses

_____ 14. Nehemiah

_____ 15. Noah

_____ 16. Samuel

_____ 17. Saul

_____ 18. Solomon

A. Conquest

B. Decline

C. Power

D. Preparation

E. Probation

F. Servitude

LESSON 10 WORKSHEET
ACROSTIC CHALLENGE

After filling out these review questions correctly, the first letters of each response will spell out the topic of today's study.

1. ☐ _ _ _ _ _ _   Old Testament book following Amos

2. ☐ _ _ _ _ _ _   Third section of New Testament books

3. ☐ _ _ _ _ _ _   Fifth period of Old Testament history

4. ☐ _ _ _ _ _   River often named with Euphrates

5. ☐ _ _ _   Old Testament book of history

6. ☐ _ _ _ _ _ _   Prominent Old Testament king

7. ☐ _ _ _ _ _ _   Two New Testament letters

8. ☐ _ _ _ _ _ _   Old Testament empire

9. ☐ _ _ _ _ _ _ _ _ _ _ Area where Adam lived

10. ☐ _ _ _ _ _   Old Testament book

11. ☐ _ _ _ _ _ _ _   He rebuilt Jerusalem's wall

12. ☐ _ _ _ _ _ _ _ _ _ _ _ _ Two more New Testament letters

13. ☐ _ _ _ _ _ _ _ _   First period of Old Testament history

14. ☐ _ _ _ _   Old Testament empire

15. ☐ _ _ _ _ _ _ _ _ _   Promise given in Genesis 3

16. ☐ _ _ _ _ _   Major Old Testament prophet

17. ☐ _ _ _ _ _ _ _ _ _ _ _ 1 of the 2 divisions of the Bible

18. ☐ _ _ _ _ _   Old Testament book of prophecy

19. ☐ _ _ _ _ _ _ _   Sixth period of Old Testament history

LESSON 16 WORKSHEET

NEW TESTAMENT GEOGRAPHY MATCH

Match each description with the location it describes.

	1. City where Jesus was born	A. Capernaum
	2. Capital of Palestine in Jesus' day	B. Bethlehem
	3. Jesus' boyhood home	C. Dead Sea
	4. Headquarters of Jesus' ministry	D. Galilee
	5. Place where Jesus was baptized	E. Jerusalem
	6. Northern province of Palestine	F. Jordan River
	7. Central province of Palestine	G. Judea
	8. Southern province of Palestine	H. Nazareth
	9. Southern sea in Palestine	I. Samaria
	10. Northern sea in Palestine	J. Sea of Galilee

LESSON 17 WORKSHEET

MORE PROPHECY AND FULFILLMENT

Match the New Testament fulfillment with the Old Testament prophecy. Use your Bible to help you.

	1. Isaiah 9:1, 2	A. Matthew 27:3-10
	2. Zechariah 9:9	B. Matthew 4:12-16
	3. Psalm 41:9	C. John 19:37
	4. Zechariah 11:12, 13	D. John 19:23, 24
	5. Psalm 22:7, 8	E. Matthew 21:4, 5
	6. Psalm 22:18	F. Matthew 27:41-43
	7. Psalm 22:16	G. John 19:36
	8. Psalm 34:20	H. John 13:18
	9. Zechariah 12:10	I. John 20:20, 25, 27
	10. Isaiah 53:9	J. Matthew 27:57-60

LESSON 18 WORKSHEET

LIFE OF JESUS

Use the keypad of your cell phone to decode the *key* events in Jesus' life. It isn't always easy, because each number stands for at least 3 possible letters!

1. Luke 2:1-20 records the 24784 of Jesus.

2. Matthew 4:1-11 records the 836782846 of Jesus.

3. Jesus cleansed the 836753 in John 2:13-16.

4. Jesus healed the son of a 66253626 in John 4:46-54.

5. Matthew 3:13-17 records Jesus' 2278476.

6. Matthew 2:19-23 tells about the 738876 from Egypt.

7. Matthew 2:1-15 tells about the 354448 to Egypt.

8. 642633687 came to Jesus at night (John 3:1-21).

9. Jesus' first 6472253 was performed in Cana of Galilee (John 2:1-11).

10. Jesus revealed who He was first to a 96626 in Samaria (John 4:1-21).

LESSON 20 WORKSHEET

WHAT HAPPENED WHEN?

Match each event from the life of Jesus with the proper period of His life.

_____ 1. Appearance to 2

_____ 2. Baptism

_____ 3. Birth

_____ 4. Calling the fishermen

_____ 5. Crucifixion

_____ 6. Feeding of 5,000

_____ 7. First miracle

_____ 8. Flight

_____ 9. Good Samaritan

_____ 10. Jairus's daughter

_____ 11. Lakeside parables

_____ 12. Lazarus

_____ 13. Little children

_____ 14. Mary's anointing

_____ 15. Nicodemus

_____ 16. Nobleman's son

_____ 17. Peter's confession

_____ 18. Rich young ruler

_____ 19. 10 virgins

_____ 20. Temptation

_____ 21. Transfiguration

_____ 22. Triumphal entry

_____ 23. Upper room

_____ 24. Woman of Samaria

_____ 25. Zaccheus

A. Preparation   E. Persecution
B. Obscurity   F. Passion Week
C. Popularity   G. Resurrection Appearances
D. Opposition

THE 12 APOSTLES

Some of Jesus' 12 apostles went by more than 1 name and had other names associated with them. In this puzzle find: Andrew, Bartholomew, Canaanite, Cephas, Iscariot, James (twice), John, Judas (twice), Lebbeus, Levi, Matthew, Nathanael, Peter, Philip, Simon (twice), son of Alpheus, son of Zebedee, Thaddeus, Thomas, Zealot. You may go backward, forward, up, down, or diagonally.

```
P  H  I  L  I  P  S  U  E  B  B  B  E  L  A  W
I  N  O  M  I  S  N  A  T  H  A  N  A  E  L
V  T  O  S  T  A  P  S  S  T  H  O  M  A  S
E  S  U  E  H  P  L  A  F  O  N  O  S  T  O
L  I  S  D  M  A  T  D  H  G  L  O  T  J  E
N  S  K  U  O  L  E  U  I  O  E  N  A  S  T
S  C  A  J  T  N  O  J  H  X  W  M  A  M  I
J  A  Z  E  A  L  O  T  S  O  E  I  A  A  N
A  R  R  O  B  E  R  W  S  S  U  O  T  T  A
M  I  S  T  H  A  D  D  E  U  S  A  O  T  A
E  O  I  O  B  N  A  A  L  L  E  N  E  H  N
S  T  S  O  N  O  F  Z  E  B  E  D  E  E  A
S  A  D  U  J  M  L  Y  H  E  L  R  L  W  C
U  L  A  P  E  I  N  S  A  H  P  E  C  X  Y
Z  N  H  O  J  S  P  E  T  E  R  W  O  E  S
```

LIFE OF PAUL

We all get ahead of ourselves sometimes. This was also true in the life of Paul. Decode these events in his life by substituting the letter of the alphabet 2 *letters before* the coded letter. (A=y, B=z, C=a, D=b, E=c, etc.)

1. ICOCNKGN was Paul's teacher (Acts 22:3).

2. Paul was born in VCTUWU (Acts 22:3).

3. Paul and Barnabas ministered in CPVKQEJ (Acts 13:1).

4. CPCPKCU baptized Paul (Acts 9:17, 18).

5. Paul was a LGY by birth (Acts 22:3).

6. Paul received a vision on the road to FCOCUEWU (Acts 9:3).

7. Paul was the apostle to the IGPVKNGU (Acts 22:21).

8. Paul first went to CTCDKC after his conversion (Galatians 1:17).

9. Paul was an CRQUVNG (Galatians 1:1).

10. DCTPCDCU introduced Paul to the other apostles in Jerusalem (Acts 9:27).

11. Paul studied the NCY of Moses (Acts 22:3).

12. Paul went by the name UCWN before he became a Christian missionary (Acts 8:1).

LESSON 26 WORKSHEET

PEOPLE, PLACES, AND BOOKS REVIEW

____ 1. Apostle who denied Jesus

____ 2. Disciple who told Peter about Jesus

____ 3. Father of the Israelites

____ 4. Leader of the Israelites

____ 5. Old Testament prophet

____ 6. Preached to the Ethiopian

____ 7. Old Testament judge

____ 8. Son of Jacob

____ 9. Persecutor turned missionary

____ 10. Third king of Israel

A. Abraham

B. Andrew

C. Elijah

D. Gideon

E. Joseph

F. Moses

G. Paul

H. Peter

I. Philip

J. Solomon

____ 1. Where God gave the 10 Commandments

____ 2. Where Elijah prayed for fire

____ 3. Capital of Judah

____ 4. Paul was imprisoned here

____ 5. Abraham's original home

____ 6. Place where Jesus was born

____ 7. Where Jesus was taken as a young child

____ 8. Where Jesus was baptized

____ 9. The Israelites crossed it

____ 10. Jesus' hometown

A. Bethlehem

B. Egypt

C. Jerusalem

D. Jordan River

E. Mount Carmel

F. Mount Sinai

G. Nazareth

H. Red Sea

I. Rome

J. Ur

____ 1. Rebuilding of Jerusalem

____ 2. Crossing of the Red Sea

____ 3. New Testament letter

____ 4. Tells of Paul's mission work

____ 5. Book of poetry

____ 6. Settling Canaan

____ 7. Creation of humankind

____ 8. Last book of the Bible

____ 9. 1 of the Gospels

____ 10. Book of prophecy

A. Acts

B. Exodus

C. Genesis

D. Isaiah

E. Joshua

F. Mark

G. Nehemiah

H. Psalms

I. Revelation

J. Romans

TRAINING FOR SERVICE EXAM 1

_____ 1. The Bible was written

A. over a period of about 1,500 years   B. by about 40 authors   C. by inspiration of God

D. all the above

_____ 2. The original languages of the Bible were

A. Hebrew and Latin   B. Greek and English   C. Hebrew and Greek   D. Arabic and Latin

_____ 3. Some manuscripts that testify to how accurately the Old Testament was copied are

A. the Satanic Verses   B. the Dead Sea Scrolls   C. the Rosetta Stone   D. A and C only

_____ 4. The Latin translation that became the official version of the Catholic Church is the

A. Vulgate   B. Textus Receptus   C. Peshitta   D. Rubicon

_____ 5. Dynamic equivalence translations like the *New Living Translation* try to translate

A. word for word   B. thought for thought   C. side by side   D. left to right

_____ 6. Knowledge about God received purely by reason and observation is

A. always wrong   B. special revelation   C. natural revelation

_____ 7. Which is *not* a division of the Old Testament?

A. Law   B. History   C. Gospels   D. Poetry   E. Prophecy

_____ 8. Which of these are listed in the order they are found in the Old Testament?

A. Isaiah, Ezekiel, Jeremiah, Daniel   B. Esther, Job, Psalms, Proverbs

_____ 9. Which is *not* a division of the New Testament?

A. Law   B. History   C. Gospels   D. Letters   E. Prophecy

_____ 10. The 4 Gospels are

A. Peter, Paul, James, John   B. Matthew, Mark, Luke, John   C. Mark, Peter, Paul, Luke

_____ 11. Most of the New Testament letters were written by

A. Jesus   B. Moses   C. Peter   D. Paul   E. John

_____ 12. What is a dispensation?

A. a plan by which God gives out His revelation   B. a form of biblical poetry

C. an act of divine condemnation   D. none of the above

_____ 13. Which is the correct order in which these dispensations occurred?

A. Christian, Patriarchal, Jewish   B. Jewish, Patriarchal, Christian   C. Patriarchal, Jewish, Christian

_____ 14. The land between the Tigris and Euphrates Rivers was called

A. Jordan   B. Mesopotamia   C. Egypt   D. Canaan

_____ 15. The main river of Canaan is the

A. Jordan   B. Tigris   C. Nile   D. Euphrates

_____ 16. Which of the following is *not* an important Old Testament mountain?

A. Nebo   B. Sinai   C. Vesuvius   D. Carmel

For questions 17–19, choose the character that is correctly matched with his period in Old Testament history.

_____ 17. A. Probation, David   B. Preparation, Noah   C. Servitude, Daniel

_____ 18. A. Conquest, Joshua   B. Power, Adam   C. Decline, Moses

_____ 19. A. Probation, Noah   B. Power, Nehemiah   C. Servitude, Abraham

_____ 20. Name 2 major world powers that arose between the Old and New Testaments.

A. Egypt and Babylon   B. Greece and Rome   C. Persia and Assyria

_____ 21. An altar demonstrated that reconciliation with God required

A. a temple   B. blood sacrifice   C. prayer   D. none of the above

For questions 22–25, match the following parts of the tabernacle with the phrase that best describes what it represented or foreshadowed. (Each will be used only once.)

A. laver   B. altar of burnt offering   C. veil   D. the court or yard

_____ 22. The sacrifice of Christ for the sins of the world

_____ 23. Christian baptism

_____ 24. Separation between Heaven and God's people on earth

_____ 25. The world

TRAINING FOR SERVICE EXAM 2

(LESSONS 14–26)

_____ 1. Which temple stood at the time of Christ?

A. Zerubbabel's temple   B. Herod's temple   C. Solomon's temple   D. Moses' temple

_____ 2. In Scripture, God did *not* directly command the building of

A. altars   B. the tabernacle   C. synagogues   D. the temple

_____ 3. Which of these festivals required Jews to travel to the temple to celebrate?

A. Pentecost   B. Purim   C. Easter   D. Hanukkah

_____ 4. The crucifixion of Jesus would take place during the feast of

A. Passover   B. Purim   C. Tabernacles   D. Hanukkah

_____ 5. In Jesus' time, what 3 main divisions of Palestine lay west of the Jordan River?

A. Egypt, Israel, Judea   B. Perea, Samaria, Judah   C. Galilee, Samaria, Judea

For questions 6–10, match the following cities with the phrase that best describes its significance in the life of Jesus. (Each will be used only once.)

A. Cana   B. Jerusalem   C. Nazareth   D. Bethlehem   E. Capernaum

_____ 6. Site of the crucifixion

_____ 7. Place of Jesus' birth

_____ 8. The headquarters of Jesus' ministry

_____ 9. Site of a wedding where Jesus performed His first miracle

_____ 10. Jesus' hometown where He spent most of His childhood

_____ 11. For the first few years of its existence, the church remained mainly in

A. Antioch   B. Jerusalem   C. Nazareth   D. Rome   E. Corinth

_____ 12. Isaiah 53 foretells Jesus coming as a

A. conquering king   B. powerful priest   C. suffering servant   D. puzzling prophet

_____ 13. Micah spoke of a coming Prince of Peace from the

A. traditions of Moses   B. town of Bethlehem   C. belly of a fish   D. root of Jesse

_____ 14. Why were the prophecies about Jesus not understood by the scholars of His time?

A. Some prophecies were obscure.   B. Some prophecies dealt with His second coming.

C. Some leaders were blinded by their own stubbornness.   D. All the above

_____ 15. Which of the following is *not* a period in the life of Christ?

A. Obscurity   B. Probation   C. Passion Week   D. Persecution

_____ 16. Which event is paired correctly with the period of Jesus' life when it happened?

A. 40 days, Jesus' baptism   B. Popularity, Sermon on the Mount   C. Opposition, birth

_____ 17. The word *apostle* means someone who

A. serves   B. is sent out   C. works miracles   D. studies

_____ 18. Which of these pairs of names does *not* refer to the same apostle?

A. Peter, Cephas   B. Andrew, Barnabas   C. Thomas, Didymus   D. Bartholomew, Nathanael

_____ 19. The command given by Jesus to His apostles in Matthew 28:19, 20 is called the

A. Great Apostasy   B. Great Commission   C. parable of the sower   D. Beatitudes

_____ 20. The writer of the book of Revelation also wrote

A. Acts   B. John   C. 1 Corinthians   D. 2 Peter

_____ 21. What did *not* occur on the Day of Pentecost following Jesus' resurrection?

A. Stephen was martyred.   B. Peter preached.   C. The apostles spoke in other languages that they had not learned.   D. About 3,000 were baptized.

_____ 22. The 2 ordinances of the church are

A. baptism and tithing   B. prayer and fasting   C. baptism and the Lord's Supper

For questions 23–25, match the person with the period of Paul's life in which he was significant. (Each will be used only once.)

A. Stephen   B. Ananias   C. Gamaliel

_____ 23. Paul the student

_____ 24. Paul the persecutor

_____ 25. Paul the convert

TRAINING FOR SERVICE FINAL EXAM

_____ 1. The Bible was written

A. over a period of about 1,500 years   B. by about 40 authors   C. by inspiration of God

D. all the above

_____ 2. The original languages of the Bible were

A. Hebrew and Latin   B. Greek and English   C. Hebrew and Greek   D. Arabic and Latin

_____ 3. Old Testament books of Law include

A. Exodus   B. Psalms   C. Numbers   D. all the above   E. A and C only

_____ 4. Old Testament books of History include

A. Joshua   B. Esther   C. 1 & 2 Kings   D. all the above   E. A and C only

_____ 5. Old Testament books of Poetry include

A. Jonah   B. Psalms   C. Leviticus   D. all the above   E. A and C only

_____ 6. Which of the following Old Testament prophets does _not_ have a book named after him?

A. Elijah   B. Jeremiah   C. Malachi   D. all the above   E. A and C only

_____ 7. Which of the following lists of Old Testament characters is in chronological order?

A. Noah, David, Abraham, Moses   B. Adam, Joshua, Solomon, Daniel

C. Abraham, Samuel, Elijah, Joseph   D. Gideon, Saul, Samuel, Isaiah

_____ 8. Which of the following lists of Old Testament events is _not_ in chronological order?

A. the fall, rule of the judges, Solomon's temple, Persian rule

B. the flood, conquest of Canaan, David's kingdom, division of the kingdom

C. the dispersion (tower of Babel), experiences in the wilderness, Saul's rise and fall, Babylonian rule

D. experiences in Egypt, fall of the southern kingdom, fall of the northern kingdom, Persian rule

_____ 9. The Gospels include

A. John   B. Peter   C. Mark   D. all the above   E. A and C only

_____ 10. The New Testament book of History is

A. Titus   B. Acts   C. Revelation   D. Hebrews   E. Philemon

_____ 11. New Testament Letters include

A. Hebrews   B. Chronicles   C. Colossians   D. all the above   E. A and C only

_____ 12. The author of the book of Revelation also wrote

A. John   B. Jeremiah   C. Acts   D. Hebrews   E. Galatians

_____ 13. Which of the following pairs of events from the life of Jesus is in chronological order?

A. visit by Nicodemus, Jesus' baptism   B. feeding 5,000, temptation of Jesus

C. transfiguration, triumphal entry   D. Mary's anointing, Peter's confession

_____ 14. Which of the following pairs of events from the life of Paul is _not_ in chronological order?

A. stoning of Stephen, trip to Rome   B. studying under Gamaliel, vision on Damascus road

C. trip to Rome, third missionary journey   D. stoning of Stephen, vision on Damascus road

_____ 15. Isaiah 53 foretold Jesus coming as a

A. conquering king   B. suffering servant   C. powerful priest   D. puzzling prophet

_____ 16. The church began during which of these Jewish festivals?

A. Passover   B. Purim   C. Pentecost   D. Hanukkah

For questions 17–20, match the following geographical areas with the letter marking its location on Map 1.

_____ 17. Mediterranean Sea

_____ 18. Mesopotamia

_____ 19. Egypt

_____ 20. Jordan River

For questions 21–25, match the following cities with the letter marking its location on Map 2.

_____ 21. Corinth

_____ 22. Rome

_____ 23. Antioch

_____ 24. Damascus

_____ 25. Jerusalem

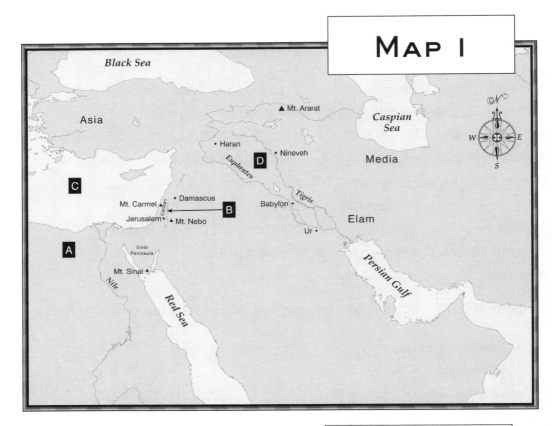

MAP 1

Black Sea

Asia

▲ Mt. Ararat

Caspian Sea

C

• Haran

Euphrates

• Nineveh

D

Media

C

Mt. Carmel ▲

• Damascus

Canaan

B

Babylon •

Tigris

Jerusalem •

▲ Mt. Nebo

Ur •

Elam

A

Sinai Peninsula

Mt. Sinai ▲

Nile

Red Sea

Persian Gulf

N
W • E
S

MAP 2

Adriatic Sea

ILLYRICUM

ITALY

A

Black Sea

MACEDONIA

THRACE

BITHYNIA

PONTUS

Philippi

Three Taverns

• Puteoli

Thessalonica •

Neapolis

Forum of Appius

• Berea

Troas

CAPPADOCIA

Aegean Sea

GALATIA

• Rhegium

ACHAIA

Athens

Ephesus

PISIDIA

• Antioch

Iconium

SICILY

B

Cenchrea

Miletus

ASIA

Lystra

Syracuse

Perga

Derbe

CILICIA

CNIDUS

Patara

PAMPHYLIA

Attalia

• Tarsus

D

RHODES

Myra

MALTA
(MELITA)

CRETE

• Lasea

Salamis

Seleucia

Fair Havens

Paphos

CYPRUS

Sidon

SYRIA

Mediterranean Sea

Tyre

E

Caesarea

N
W • E
S

• Cyrene

CYRENE

C

JUDEA

Dead Sea

Alexandria •

EGYPT

Nile

0   80   160   240

ANSWERS FOR *TRAINING FOR SERVICE* EXAMS

ANSWERS FOR EXAM 1 (LESSONS 1–13)

1. D	6. C	11. D	16. C	21. B
2. C	7. C	12. A	17. C	22. B
3. B	8. B	13. C	18. A	23. A
4. A	9. A	14. B	19. A	24. C
5. B	10. B	15. A	20. B	25. D

ANSWERS FOR EXAM 2 (LESSONS 14–26)

1. B	6. B	11. B	16. B	21. A
2. C	7. D	12. C	17. B	22. C
3. A	8. E	13. B	18. B	23. C
4. A	9. A	14. D	19. B	24. A
5. C	10. C	15. B	20. B	25. B

ANSWERS FOR FINAL EXAM

1. D	6. A	11. E	16. C	21. B
2. C	7. B	12. A	17. C	22. A
3. E	8. D	13. C	18. D	23. D
4. D	9. E	14. C	19. A	24. E
5. B	10. B	15. B	20. B	25. C

Certificate of Completion

THIS IS TO CERTIFY THAT

_____

HAS SUCCESSFULLY COMPLETED THE 26-SESSION BIBLE SURVEY COURSE

AND EXAMINATION REQUIREMENTS OF

TRAINING *for* SERVICE

TRAINING
for
SERVICE

Standard
PUBLISHING
Bringing The Word to Life

_____
COURSE FACILITATOR

_____
DATE

OVER ONE MILLION TRAINED

TRAINING
for
SERVICE

A BASIC BIBLE OVERVIEW
FOR EVERY CHRISTIAN

26-SESSION CERTIFICATION PROGRAM

Standard®
PUBLISHING
Bringing The Word to Life
Cincinnati, Ohio

Published by Standard Publishing, Cincinnati, Ohio
www.standardpub.com

Copyright © 1907, 1934, 1942, 1964, 1983, 1998, 2011 by Standard Publishing

Also available: *Training for Service Leader Guide*, ISBN 978-0-7847-3300-4, copyright © 2011 by Standard Publishing

Printed in: United States of America
Authors: Jim Eichenberger, 2011; Eleanor Daniel, 1983; Orrin Root, 1964; Cecil James (C. J.) Sharp, 1934; Herbert Moninger, 1907
Project editor: Lynn Lusby Pratt
Cover design: Faceout Studio
Interior design: Dina Sorn at Ahaa! Design

All Scripture quotations—as well as the spellings of names, places, and scriptural terms—are taken from the *King James Version* of the Bible.

ISBN 978-0-7847-3301-1

16 15 14 13 12 11   1 2 3 4 5 6 7 8 9

FOREWORD

For over a century, *Training for Service* has equipped more than 1 million volunteers with this basic course and certification for Bible teaching. Ideal for those planning to teach Sunday school, serve as church leaders, or facilitate small groups, it is also recommended for anyone who just wants a Bible 101 course.

In the first edition of the book, author Herbert Moninger wrote:

> *The studies composing this book were originally given before the members of the Northside Union Teacher-training Class in Cincinnati, O., 122 of whom passed a successful examination and received diplomas from the Ohio Sunday-school Association. If this book has any value, it will largely be because these lessons were tested before being printed* (preface, 1907 edition).

Educator and author C. J. Sharp revised Moninger's original *Training for Service* in 1934. Sharp followed the general outlines of the original and retained the book's practical, biblical goals. Sharp said:

> *"New Training for Service" is offered to Bible-school teachers and workers as an answer to the widespread demand for a practical teacher-training book suited to the average teacher. . . . The teacher of the Bible should first have a good general knowledge of the Bible itself and the foundation principles of pedagogy as applied to the teaching of the Bible* (foreword, 1934 edition).

Orrin Root, an editor, writer, and Christian educator, authored the second major revision of *Training for Service.* He responded to requests for a shorter, more specialized study and explained:

> *Moninger's original plan of Bible study has been retained, but has been distilled to 26 lessons filled with factual and illustrative materials, Scripture readings, and questions for discussion and review* (preface, 1964 edition).

Dr. Eleanor Daniel updated Mr. Root's revision. This respected seminary professor and Christian educator enhanced *Training for Service* with complete lesson plans, assignments, and classroom activities. She also:

> *. . . updated the information on Bible translations, added a history of the period between the testaments, and [gave] the book a new look* (foreword, 1983 edition).

This current revision has been done with the understanding that we are but the proverbial "dwarfs standing on the shoulders of giants." The general structure of past revisions has been retained, but content has been revised to reflect the best current understanding of the Bible, education, and the questions being asked in the 21st century. Furthermore, computer technology has allowed us to provide even more features at www.trainingforservice.com. It is to the time-tested heritage of *Training for Service* and the goal of seeing more generations become competent Christian educators that this revision is dedicated.

—Jim Eichenberger, 2011

CONTENTS

HOW TO USE THIS BOOK 6

THE BIBLE

1. HOW WE GOT OUR BIBLE 8
2. GOD'S WORD TO US 14
3. DIVISIONS OF THE BIBLE 18
4. BOOKS OF THE OLD TESTAMENT 22
5. BOOKS OF THE NEW TESTAMENT 26

OLD TESTAMENT GEOGRAPHY AND HISTORY

6. 3 DISPENSATIONS 29
7. THE OLD TESTAMENT WORLD 32
8. OLD TESTAMENT PEOPLE—PART 1 35
9. OLD TESTAMENT PEOPLE—PART 2 38
10. OLD TESTAMENT PERIODS—PART 1 41
11. OLD TESTAMENT PERIODS—PART 2 43
12. OLD TESTAMENT PERIODS—PART 3 45
    Between the Testaments 48

OLD TESTAMENT INSTITUTIONS

13. ALTAR AND TABERNACLE 51

14. TEMPLE AND SYNAGOGUE 54

15. THE JEWISH FEASTS 57

THE CHRIST

16. NEW TESTAMENT LANDS 61

17. THE CHRIST IN PROPHECY 65

18. LIFE OF CHRIST—PART 1 68

19. LIFE OF CHRIST—PART 2 71

20. LIFE OF CHRIST—PART 3 74

THE CHURCH

21. THE APOSTLES AND THE GREAT COMMISSION 77

22. BEGINNINGS OF THE CHURCH 79

23. NEW LIFE IN CHRIST 82

24. LIFE OF PAUL—PART 1 85

25. LIFE OF PAUL—PART 2 88

26. THE BIBLE FOR THE WHOLE WORLD 91

PRONUNCIATION GUIDE 94

BIBLIOGRAPHY 95

— HOW TO USE THIS BOOK—

Training for Service has proved to be immensely popular among church leaders since its first publication in 1907. It appeals to thousands of Christians who are enthusiastic about the help it gives them in their Bible study.

What differentiates *Training for Service* from just another Sunday school or small group study is its distinctly academic approach. That is not to say that it is beyond the capabilities of the average adult believer. In fact, just the opposite is true. But while the study is not marked by its difficulty, there are expectations to be met by the participant.

STUDENT PARTICIPATION

It is assumed that a *Training for Service* study will be taken seriously. The first requirement is regular attendance. Each session is built on another, so missing a lesson will leave the participant ill equipped for the following lesson. If a situation arises that makes it necessary for a student to miss a session, he or she is encouraged to contact the leader and make arrangements to find out what was missed.

Furthermore, pre-class preparation is a must. Each student is expected to study the lesson material before class and come to each session ready to participate in the discussion. At times, additional assignments may be given to some or all students before class.

MEMORIZATION AND REVIEW

The place of memory work in education is much smaller than it used to be. Yet we know that it is still necessary to learn the alphabet, for example, for without it one can hardly use a dictionary or a telephone directory.

For similar reasons, you will learn the names of the books of the Bible, in order, so that you can quickly find a passage when you want it. When you have learned to name the leading Bible characters in order, you will ever after know that Moses comes later than Joseph and earlier than David. This book has other lists to be memorized. They are the ABCs of Bible study. It will not take long to learn them, and they will be a lifelong help in studying Scripture.

TESTS AND CERTIFICATION

From its introduction a century ago, *Training for Service* has been used to ensure that church leaders and teachers have at least a baseline understanding of Scripture. Certificates stating that graduates have gained that knowledge have been available throughout the history of the book.

The basis for issuing certificates is testing. Therefore, 3 tests—1 on lessons 1–13, 1 on lessons 14–26, and a final exam—are a part of this course. The leader of the lessons is in charge of administering these tests.

INDEPENDENT STUDY

Training for Service is designed for a classroom setting. The course counts on the interaction of students with the leader and with one another for optimum learning.

Nevertheless, church volunteers are busy people, so flexibility is necessary. If a *Training for*

Service class is not available, an individual may complete this course as an independent study. That person may choose a teacher, minister, or other qualified person to administer the final exam and grade it. The person selected will sign and present a certificate to the student who has received a grade of 70 percent or more on the final exam. The final exam, answers for the exam, and a certificate master are included in *Training for Service Leader Guide*.

HELPFUL RESOURCES

You will need a Bible and your own copy of *Training for Service Student Guide*. In addition, some other resources will help you in this study.

1. *Multiple translations*. *Training for Service* is designed so that it may be used with the teacher's and students' preferred Bible translation. But since the Bible was not written in English, comparing a Scripture passage in a variety of translations can help in understanding.

2. *Concordance*. A Bible concordance is similar to an index in a book. By looking up a word in a concordance, the places in the Bible where the word is used may be found. Many Bibles include an abridged concordance that shows some uses of each word listed. A complete concordance can be purchased as a separate volume. There are also analytical concordances that show places where a particular word of the original language is used, even if it has multiple meanings in English.

3. *Bible atlas, Bible dictionary, Bible encyclopedia*. These Bible references serve a similar function to their secular counterparts and will give further insight into the geography, history, and customs of Bible times. The classic *Halley's Bible Handbook* is probably the most familiar. Standard Publishing offers 2 ideal, inexpensive resources in this category:

- *Standard Bible Atlas* (ISBN 978-0-7847-1872-8) has 31 full-color maps, 14 charts, and 5 reproducible map masters.
- *Standard Bible Dictionary* (ISBN 978-0-7847-1873-5) is a concise pronunciation guide of more than 2,000 Bible words, with easy-to-understand definitions.

4. *Online resources*. Many Web sites are dedicated to providing Bible study resources. Some of the most helpful are:

- Bible Gateway—www.biblegateway.com
- Biblos—www.biblos.com
- Bible Study Tools—www.biblestudytools.com

[handwritten note:] INSPIRATION: God's Revelation COMMUNICATED to us THROUGH WRITERS who used their own words/minds, yet God so directed their lives and thoughts that the words they used in writing were the very words of God.

HOW WE GOT OUR BIBLE

——— ORIGIN OF THE BIBLE ———

A. DIVINE SOURCE

You would not be participating in this course unless you have come to believe that the Bible is a unique book that comes from God. It is reasonable to assume that a loving God would communicate to humankind and that He would place this communication in an objective form that could be handed down and preserved from generation to generation. It is also reasonable to believe that by examining purported holy books, a book truly from God would stand out from among them. Other books make these cases, but through this study you will most likely be strengthened in the conviction that the Bible is divine in its source and is unlike any other book.

B. HUMAN WRITERS

1. *Who and when?* Today we often use the word *prophet* to refer to someone who tells the future. But in the biblical sense, a prophet is someone who speaks or writes a message from God. God used about 40 such prophets in writing the Bible over a period from approximately 1400 BC to AD 100.

2. *Source of the content.* Some of the writers simply passed on what God had told them, as when Moses wrote the law (Deuteronomy 31:24) or when preaching prophets proclaimed their messages (Nahum 1:1; Habakkuk 1:1; Zephaniah 1:1, to name a few). Some of them wrote what they had seen, as when disciples of Jesus recorded what was done in their presence (2 Peter 1:16; 1 John 1:1-3). Some sought out trustworthy, historical accounts. Moses wrote centuries after the events found in the book of Genesis, so he certainly may have used sources dating from those days. Luke was not an eyewitness to the ministry of Jesus, but wrote only after careful research (Luke 1:1-4). Paul included words commonly recited or sung in the early church (1 Corinthians 15:3-5; 2 Timothy 2:11-13). But in every case, all of them were guided by a single mind—the mind of God (2 Timothy 3:16, 17; 2 Peter 1:21).

3. *Incidental content.* Just as authors do today, these human writers made references to other writings and sayings of the day (2 Samuel 1:18; Jude 14, 15). That does *not* mean that everything in those sources is inspired and is equal to Scripture. Jesus, for example, quoted a children's song (Matthew 11:17) and proverbs about predicting the weather (Matthew 16:2, 3). Paul even quoted an inscription from an idol and the words of pagan poets to make his point (Acts 17:23, 28). Cultural references show that the books were written at the time the events occurred, not centuries later.

C. PRESERVED THROUGH CENTURIES

1. This lesson is a study of how the Bible has been *transmitted* to us after it was written. How do we know the Bible we have today is the Word as originally written?

2. God inspired the original writers so that they could not make mistakes. But both copyists and translators *could* and *did* make errors. Since many ancient manuscripts and translations have been preserved, we can find when these mistakes have been made.

——— ANCIENT MANUSCRIPTS ——— AND VERSIONS

While we have no part of the Bible in the handwriting of the original authors, we have 2 kinds of sources from which we can learn what they wrote. These are manuscripts and versions.

A. DEFINITIONS

1. *Manuscripts* are documents written by hand. Before printing was invented, this was the only way of producing books. We have no Bible manuscripts written by the original authors, but we have thousands of copies written by hand in the same language they used.

2. A *version* is a translation of any document into another language. Some ancient versions were translated from manuscripts older than any we now have. Therefore, they help us to know just what the original writers wrote.

B. OLD TESTAMENT SCRIPTURES

1. *Manuscripts.* The Old Testament books were written in the Hebrew language between 1400 BC and 400 BC. They were collected and preserved by the Jewish priesthood. After the last Old Testament prophet (Malachi), a group of priests we call the scribes painstakingly copied, preserved, and studied these manuscripts

Until the middle of the 20th century, the oldest Old Testament manuscripts available were the Masoretic texts, copies made by a group of Jews known as the Masoretes between the 7th and 10th centuries AD. But in 1947, scrolls written around 100 BC were discovered. These Dead Sea Scrolls agree with the Masoretic texts, showing the remarkable accuracy with which they were preserved and copied.

2. *Versions.* The oldest version of the Old Testament is a Greek version called the Septuagint (pronounced Sep-*too*-ih-jent). From the Latin word for 70, this name was given because the translation was made by about 70 Jewish scholars in Alexandria, Egypt, around 250 BC. Ancient versions in Syriac, Egyptian, Ethiopic, Armenian, and other languages also exist.

C. NEW TESTAMENT SCRIPTURES

1. *Manuscripts.* All the books of the New Testament were written in Greek during the first century after Christ. Shortly after they were written, churches began to collect manuscripts of Paul's letters and other writings that they recognized (through the Holy Spirit working within them) to be inspired. Early church councils would later confirm which books and letters were part of the New Testament, but they were *not* creating the New Testament canon (collection). They were simply affirming what was known as the books were written.

Manuscripts were written on papyrus (pressed pulp of reeds) and later on animal skins. Because of the delicate nature of papyrus, only fragments of the earliest manuscripts exist today. A fragment of papyrus known as Rylands Library Papyrus P52 was discovered in 1920. P52 contains portions from the Gospel of John and is the oldest New Testament portion known today. It was copied around AD 125, less than 40 years after John wrote his Gospel!

Parchment (animal skin) manuscripts were collected and bound into books called codices. The earliest manuscript collections are Codex Sinaiticus and Codex Vaticanus and are both from around AD 350. In all, over 5,000 complete or fragmented Greek manuscripts exist, a testimony to how well the New Testament has been preserved and accurately copied.

2. *Versions.* The Bible was translated into Syriac and called the Peshitta, meaning "simple version." This probably occurred in the first half of the 2nd century. Shortly thereafter, the Greek was translated into the Latin. A more careful Latin version was completed about AD 400. Translated by Jerome and called the Vulgate (which means "common," or "popular"), this version became the official Bible of the Roman Catholic Church and of western Europe. Probably in the 3rd and 4th centuries, versions were made also in Coptic (Egyptian), Gothic, Ethiopic, and Armenian. Made from very ancient manuscripts, all of these help us to be sure the Bible we have is essentially the same as the original writings. It also shows the desire of the church from the earliest days to have a translation of the Bible that is easily understood by all.

——— ENGLISH VERSIONS ———

A. OLD ENGLISH VERSIONS

There were people in the British Isles in the early days of the church, but the English language developed later. There was an early need for God's Word in the native tongue.

1. *Anglo-Saxon.* In 735, Bede, then at the point of death, finished his translation of John's Gospel into Anglo-Saxon, 1 of the languages from which English developed.

2. *Middle English.* In the 11th century, William of Normandy conquered England. In the course of time, the Norman-French language blended with the Anglo-Saxon to become what is sometimes called Middle English. About 1380, Wycliffe and his coworkers translated the Bible into Middle English from the Latin Vulgate, which was the official Bible of the church in that time. The Roman Catholic Church denounced Wycliffe as a heretic.

3. *Early Modern English.* In 1525, William Tyndale became the first to translate directly from the original Greek and Hebrew. Myles Coverdale translated the Scriptures in 1535 from the Vulgate and Luther's German translation, using Tyndale's work to guide him. Other translations followed, all strongly influenced by Tyndale. Because the printing press was in use, the Scriptures were distributed more widely than ever before, and opposition grew from those demanding that the Vulgate be the only acceptable translation. The Roman Catholic Church executed Tyndale as a heretic.

Mary Tudor came to the throne and brought England again under the power of the Roman Church, persecuting Protestants so strongly as to earn the name Bloody Mary. Some of the best English scholars fled to continental Europe. In Geneva in 1560, William Whittington and others completed the *Geneva Bible*, based largely on earlier English versions. It was dedicated to Mary's more tolerant successor, Elizabeth I. Some of the *Geneva Bible* offended the bishops of the Church of England. They responded by publishing the *Bishops' Bible* in 1568.

Through the rest of the 16th century, the clergymen used the *Bishops' Bible*; but the *Geneva Bible* was preferred by many of the people, especially the Puritans, who were intent on reforming the church. The *Geneva Bible* was the first English translation used in colonial America.

The rise in popularity of English translations helped convince the Catholic Church to prepare a translation. The *Douay-Rheims Bible* was translated from the Vulgate and completed in 1610.

It is still considered the English Bible of choice by traditional Catholics.

4. The *King James Version*. In 1604, King James appointed a committee of 54 scholars to prepare a new version. They followed the *Bishops' Bible* except where they thought changes were needed; but they consulted other English translations, the German translation, the Greek and Hebrew texts, the Syriac, the Septuagint, and several Latin versions. The result of their labors was the *King James Version*, published in 1611 and still the most-used Bible in the English language.

B. Revised versions

1. Any living language is constantly changing. Many words used in the *King James Version* (such as *neesings, besom,* and *wist*) are now almost unknown. Other words have changed their meanings. For example, *let* (Romans 1:13) formerly meant "to hinder," but now it means "to permit." *Conversation* now means "talk," but to the English people of King James's day it meant "behavior." Also, older and presumably more reliable Greek manuscripts not available to *King James Version* translators had since been discovered.

2. In the course of centuries, therefore, scholars began to see a need to revise the *King James Version*. In 1885, a committee of 51 British scholars, assisted by 32 Americans, produced the *Revised Version*. In 1901, the American members of the committee brought out the *American Standard Version*, introducing some variations more in accord with American usage of English.

C. Modern English versions

Translation of ancient languages is more than substituting each word for another. First of all, a language no longer in use has to be learned by comparing ancient manuscripts in that language. In that way scholars learn multiple meanings of words and figures of speech. Also, different languages use different word order in sentences.

An interlinear translation (which places the Greek or Hebrew text on a line with the English equivalent right below it) shows the differences in sentence structure between languages. An interlinear translation would render the familiar first words of John 3:16 as: "So for loved the God the world that the Son only begotten gave." It is obvious that true translation is more than "decoding"! But there are differing ideas as to what makes the best Bible translation. (A chart showing popular translations and the type of translation each is can be found on page 13.)

1. *Formal equivalence*. This type of translation attempts to substitute English words for their Hebrew or Greek counterparts as much as possible, while placing the words in a readable English sentence structure.

2. *Dynamic equivalence*. Other scholars believe that the best translations are not word for word, but rather thought for thought. A dynamic equivalence translation will try to keep the paragraph order the same, but will not show concern for a 1-to-1 correspondence of words. A dynamic equivalence translation that may group verses together and use modern idioms is generally called a paraphrase.

3. *Optimal equivalence*. Both of the above ideas have merits and drawbacks. Optimal equivalence describes a translation that tries to balance between both theories of translation in order to most accurately convey the meaning of the text without taking liberties with the original languages.

MAIN IDEAS OF THIS LESSON

The Bible is unique because it alone is authored by ___God___.

About _40_ human authors wrote the Bible over a period of roughly _1500_ years.

Most of the Old Testament was written in ___Hebrew___, while most of the New Testament was written in ___GREEK___.

The ___VULGATE___ is the name of a Latin translation that became the official Bible of the Roman Catholic Church.

Three theories of Bible translations are:

deep bible study
FORMAL / LITERAL → *deep bible study* equivalence *emphasizes original language wording / order ; maintains historical distance*

childrens; simple questions! elderly
DYNAMIC / FREE / PARAPHRASE equivalence : *simplicity / clarity of translated word over precision*

evangelism preaching)
OPTIMAL / FUNCTIONAL equivalence : *finding equivalent concepts in translation language*

QUESTIONS FOR DEEPER CONSIDERATION AND DISCUSSION

1. Both Islam and the Church of Jesus Christ of Latter-Day Saints offer so-called holy books that claim to be more accurate than the Bible. In each case, the book was delivered by 1 man who lived centuries after many of the events described in the book. From what you have learned about the human authors of the Bible, how would you respond to such claims?

The Bible is authored by God as the source while using 40 authors in whom many have copied word for word, whereas other texts like Kuran / Book of morman came from an individual

2. We have no Bible books in the handwriting of their authors. What 2 kinds of documents do we have? Distinguish between them and explain how they help us know what was in the books as they were originally written. *Manuscripts & versions.*
Original language copies → translations written by hand

3. Why was the discovery of the Dead Sea Scrolls in 1947 so significant? What are some of the earliest New Testament manuscripts in existence? How do these discoveries make us even more confident that the Bible has been accurately copied throughout the centuries? *Scrolls showed accuracy! No discrepancies*

4. Why is translating from ancient languages more complicated than simply substituting each word for another? Briefly describe the 3 basic theories of modern Bible translation. What are some strengths and weaknesses of each theory? Do you think it is best to use a single translation of the Bible when studying? Why or why not? *Multiple meanings of words, figures of speech, & word order.*

Dynamic :

5.) Is there such a thing as an inspired translation? Only original manuscripts!

POPULAR ENGLISH BIBLE TRANSLATIONS

Version	Date	Grade Level*	Translation Type**	Comments
King James Version	Began 1604, completed 1611	12th	Formal equivalence	The most commonly used text of the *King James Version* is Standard Text of 1769.
Douay-Rheims Bible	NT, 1609 OT, 1610	10th	Formal equivalence	English translation from the Vulgate by the Catholic Church
American Standard Version	1901	12th	Formal equivalence	Essentially a revision of the *King James Version*
Revised Standard Version	NT, 1946 OT, 1952	7th	Formal equivalence with some dynamic equivalence	A revision of the *American Standard Version;* first version to refer to the Dead Sea Scrolls in translating the Old Testament
The Living Bible	NT, 1962 OT, 1971	8th	Dynamic equivalence/ paraphrase	Kenneth Taylor attempted to paraphrase the *American Standard Version* in a language suitable for children
New American Standard Bible	NT, 1963 OT, 1971	11th	Formal equivalence	Generally thought of as being the closest to a word-for-word translation
Good News Translation (Today's English Version)	NT, 1966 OT, 1974	7th	Dynamic equivalence	Limited-vocabulary translation originally for those who spoke English as a second language
New International Version	NT, 1973 OT, 1978	7th	Optimal equivalence	Often considered the middle ground between formal and dynamic versions
New King James Version	1982	8th	Formal equivalence	Uses the same manuscripts as the *King James Version*
The Message	NT, 1993 OT, 2002	7th	Dynamic equivalence/ paraphrase	Eugene Peterson attempted to retain the flavor of the original languages in everyday English
New Living Translation	1996	6th–7th	Dynamic equivalence	Beginning as a revision to *The Living Bible,* scholars went to the original languages to produce a true translation
English Standard Version	2001	8th	Formal equivalence	Rivals the *New American Standard Bible* as a literal translation, but more readable

* Estimated from different samples of the translations. Estimates may differ in other summaries and charts.
** Evaluation made from translators' notes, using definitions on page 11 of this book.

LESSON 2

GOD'S WORD TO US

—— WE NEED TO KNOW! ——

Knowledge is essential. In whatever situation we may be, we need to know the truth about what is expected in that situation and the authority governing it. Without this kind of knowledge, a baseball game would become a riot, an army would become a mob, and a nation could not exist. We would expect that a loving God would reveal all vital knowledge to humankind. He does so in 2 ways.

A. GOD IS THE SOURCE OF NATURAL REVELATION

1. *Definition.* Natural (also called general) revelation is that knowledge available to anyone simply by living in this world. This includes:

- that which can be directly experienced by our senses. We see that the sky is blue, taste that sugar is sweet, and feel that sandpaper is rough.
- that which is deduced from observation and human reason. Humankind has come to understand natural laws that consistently operate in our world. In that way we can know the time of the sunrise, the position of the planets, or the source of diseases.
- that which human beings seem to instinctively know outside the realm of physical senses. While it may be hard to explain, human beings are recognized to have a conscience. We somehow sense that certain behaviors are right or wrong.

2. *The value of natural revelation.* Human beings from anywhere in the world can conclude that there must be some powerful, orderly, and moral force in the universe (see Psalm 19:1-6; Romans 1:19, 20).

3. *The limitations of natural revelation.* While natural revelation has great value, it is incomplete. The findings of scientists such as Newton, Darwin, and Einstein are valuable when they deal with direct observation. But those observations must be separated from their conclusions. For example, speculation about how life might have begun or come to its current forms can blur the line between science and philosophy. Writings of philosophers and literary figures such as Confucius, Mohammed, Plato, Milton, and Shakespeare express some universal desires of humankind but are also mixed with biases from their cultural backgrounds. The human conscience and intuition can be disabled by past experiences, psychological disorders, or a practice of consistently overriding it by force of the will.

B. GOD IS THE SOURCE OF SPECIAL REVELATION

1. *Definition.* Special revelation is that which comes directly from God and not from natural sources. Christians hold that the Bible is the only source of *absolutely certain* special revelation. It was written by inspired men, men specially guided by God's Spirit so that they

wrote just what God wanted them to write, without error. Through the Bible, God answers questions that cannot be adequately addressed by natural revelation:

- *Who is God?* (see Genesis 17:1; Exodus 34:6, 7; John 3:16).
- *How did we get here?* (see Genesis 1, 2; Psalm 104:1-24; John 1:1-3).
- *What are we doing here?* (see Ecclesiastes 12:13; Micah 6:8; Matthew 5–7).
- *What is our ultimate fate?* (see Mark 16:15, 16; Matthew 25:31-46; 2 Peter 3:10-14; Revelation 21:1–22:7).

2. *The purpose of special revelation.* Many purposes may be suggested, but none are more important than these:

- *To help us know God.* If we come to know the Book but do not come to know God, we have failed and the purpose of God has been defeated (see Jeremiah 24:7). *Knowing Bible vs "" "" God.*
- *To guide our lives.* If we come to know the Book but do not come to live by the Book, this too is failure (see James 1:22).

WE NEED TO UNDERSTAND AND PRACTICE WHAT WE LEARN

God has given His Word, but it has no effect in our lives unless it actually comes *to us*—unless we receive it, study it, understand it, and obey it. It deserves not just our study, but our *reverent study*. Those who approach it with a skeptical or faultfinding attitude may miss its treasures. Those who read it as a message from God will be richly rewarded.

Yet God delivered His Word in book form. We must not ignore the basic rules we follow when reading any other book. The Bible is a book like no other, but it is *still* a book!

A. KEEP IT IN CONTEXT

We would never think of taking a few words or phrases from any other book and using them to prove a point. We hate it when someone tries to use our words that way! We recognize that we must understand words within the context of the work by asking some key questions:

1. *Who says?* Here is a sentence we would not expect to find in the Bible: "There is no God." The sentence is found in Psalm 14:1, but it is attributed to a foolish person. What a difference that makes! Oftentimes God's Word quotes the word of someone other than God. For example, Genesis 3:4, 5 quotes a lie of the serpent, directly contradicting a statement from God in Genesis 2:17. Job's friends made many statements about God that God later refuted (Job 42:7-9). A man born blind repeated the common wisdom that God does not hear the prayer of sinners (John 9:31), but elsewhere in Scripture the truth of the matter is revealed (1 John 1:8, 9).

2. *Who's being addressed?* The angel's announcement in Luke 1:26-33 was spoken to Mary, but the teaching of Romans 12 was given to all the Christians in Rome. The announcement to Mary cannot be applied to anyone else, but the instructions in Romans 12 are for all Christians everywhere. Ephesians 5:22–6:9 has messages directed especially to wives, husbands, children, fathers, servants, and masters of that day but is undoubtedly intended for all Christian families, employees, and employers to this day.

3. *Did a command mean something in the original culture that it does not mean today?* Paul once wrote to Timothy, "Use a little wine for thy stomach's sake and thine often infirmities" (1 Timothy 5:23). Doubtless this was excellent advice under the circumstances, but it can hardly be applied to anyone else unless he has the same stomach trouble Timothy had—and even then it may be that a better medicine is available under present circumstances.

4. *Does it matter when the command was given?* Yes! A distinction is to be made between the Old Testament and the New Testament, especially when it comes to issues of salvation. The Old Testament foretold a new and different covenant (Jeremiah 31:31-34); the book of Hebrews explains at length that this new and better covenant has replaced the old. We are under the new covenant, not the law of the Old Testament. Therefore, laws about food, clothing, and sacrifices found in the law must be understood as commands from the old covenant.

Early in the history of the church, an effort was made to bring all Christians under the Old Testament law, but Christian leaders, guided by the Holy Spirit, rejected that attempt (Acts 15:1-29). We can safely follow their example and reject a similar attempt whenever it is made. Nevertheless, it is profitable to study the Old Testament as well as the New (2 Timothy 3:16, 17; 1 Corinthians 10:11). The Old helps us understand the New (Galatians 3:24, 25); it tells much about our Savior (Isaiah 53); it helps us to know God (Exodus 34:6, 7); and it helps to guide our living (Micah 6:8).

B. READ THE WHOLE BOOK

Scripture does not contradict itself. Therefore, we must let Scripture interpret Scripture and not think a single passage is complete in and of itself. An example may be seen in the answers given to people seeking salvation. One person was told to believe in Jesus (Acts 16:30, 31), others were told to repent and be baptized (2:37, 38), and another was told to be baptized and wash away his sins (22:16). But when we study further, we see that there is no contradiction or confusion here. Each person was told what he should do at that particular time. When we know the whole story, it is plain that all the converts believed, repented, and were baptized.

C. GOD IS A GREAT AUTHOR

Good authors write with style and variety. Would we not expect the same of a book authored by God himself? Of course we would!

1. *Figures of speech.* We know that when someone says, "Draw the drapes," he does not mean that we should take out pencil and paper and make a sketch! We understand that *40 winks* and *sawing logs* are metaphors for sleep and should be taken as such. Likewise, we should be aware that figures of speech are used in the Bible. For example, in ancient times the firstborn son in a family had special authority. When the Bible refers to Jesus as the firstborn (Colossians 1:15; Hebrews 1:6), we should not take that to mean that Jesus did not exist and at some point was born. The phrase is a metaphor referring to Jesus' supreme authority.

2. *Differing types of literature.* The Bible is actually a library of books. And as in any good library, there are different types of literature. The Bible contains books of history, poetry, letters, and more. When we read a poem that describes our beloved as a flower, we recognize that we are describing a person of delicacy and beauty. Likewise, when in a song the poet refers to God's Word as a light (Psalm 119:105, for example), we do not look for a place in our Bible to insert batteries! We recognize that when we say, "Early to bed and early to rise, makes a man healthy, wealthy, and wise," we are reciting a proverb that is a generalization. When we happen to meet a person who has great sleeping patterns but is poor or ill, we do not see that as disproving the proverb. In the same proverbial fashion, the Bible tells us that when parents properly train their children, they will not stray from the truth (Proverbs 22:6). A single incident of a misbehaving adult child does not disprove this proverb or necessarily show the parents to be lacking.

MAIN IDEAS OF THIS LESSON

God is the source of all knowledge—both __NATURAL__ revelation and __SPECIAL__ revelation.

Natural revelation clearly demonstrates that there must be some __Powerful__, __orderly__, and __moral force__ force in the universe.

While natural revelation has great value, it is __INCOMPLETE__.

Special revelation is that which comes directly from __GOD__ and not from __NATURAL__ sources.

Special revelation is given to help us __KNOW__ God and to __GUIDE__ our lives.

When reading the Bible we must understand words within the __CONTEXT__ of the work.

QUESTIONS FOR DEEPER CONSIDERATION AND DISCUSSION

1. List some sources of natural revelation and the value and limitations of each source.
   1.) Sensory experiences, 2.) observation / human reasoning, & 3.) human conscience

2. List some questions beyond the scope of natural revelation. Why do you believe they are vital questions nonetheless? 1.) Who is God? 2.) How did we get here? 3.) What are we doing here? 4.) What is our ultimate fate?
   These are the questions humanity longs to understand! "There is a God shaped vacuum in the ♡ of every man which cannot be filled by any created thing, but only by God, the Creator, made known through Jesus.

3. Many religions focus on knowing about God (or gods) or knowing what God requires. What are some differences between these ideas and actually knowing God? What does that say about the relationship the God of the Bible wants to have with humankind? Knowing God & knowing things about Him is two totally different things.

4. Tell about a time when you have been quoted out of context. How might people quote God out of context? Give 1 or 2 examples.

5. Give 1 or 2 examples of how a certain Scripture may help us understand another.

6. Give 1 or 2 examples of how recognizing literary styles and devices helps us understand Scripture correctly.
   • Prophecy
   • Wisdom/poetry: Figurative

DIVISIONS OF THE BIBLE

Though usually bound in a single volume, the Bible is really a collection of 66 books. The significance of this can be seen by comparing this collection with a home library.

Suppose I have 1,000 books on history, poetry, science, mathematics, geography, and theology. They have information on practically every subject. Then suppose I want to know something about the Vietnam War, so I reach for the nearest book. If it is a book of poetry, I may read it all without finding what I want. I should have selected a book of American history.

Now suppose I want to know how to become a Christian. I am sure the information is in the Bible. So I open the Bible and start to read. If I happen to be reading the book of Joshua, I can read a long time and fail to find the information I want, because I am reading Old Testament history, a record of the times before salvation in Christ was offered. For that reason, it is important to be aware of how the Bible is divided and what each division contains.

The 2 largest divisions of the Bible are the Old Testament and the New Testament. The Old Testament has 39 books, and the New Testament has 27 books. As discussed earlier in this study, about 40 different writers wrote these books over a period of about 1,500 years. It is also important to note that the books in each large division are not always arranged chronologically. Instead, they are arranged by the type of literature each is.

—— DIVISIONS OF THE ——
OLD TESTAMENT

The books of the Old Testament fall naturally into 4 groups, which are easily memorized: Law (5 books), History (12 books), Poetry (5 books), and Prophecy (17 books). (5-$2 - 55-12

A. EXCEPTIONS TO THE CLASSIFICATION

The names assigned to the 4 divisions give a general idea of what is in them, but no division is limited to 1 kind of literature. For example, the books of Law also contain history, poetry, and prophecy; the books of History and Poetry have prophecy too; and the books of Prophecy have much history and poetry.

B. THE MESSAGE OF EACH DIVISION

1. *The books of Law* are the first 5 books of the Bible. You may also hear them referred to as the Pentateuch (meaning "5 books") or the Torah (although this term can also refer to the entire Old Testament). They trace God's dealing with mankind from the creation of the world; through the flood of Noah's time; through the beginning of the Hebrew nation in Abraham, Isaac, and Jacob; through their escape from Egypt and their wandering in the wilderness, to the time when Moses died and his people were ready to enter the promised land with Joshua as their leader.

All this history provides the setting in which God gave the Hebrew people the law that fills a large part of this group of books. This is sometimes called the Jewish law or the Old Testament law or the law of Moses (Mosaic law). The best-known parts of it are the 10 Commandments (Exodus 20:3-17), the greatest of all commandments (Deuteronomy 6:5), and the commandment second in importance (Leviticus 19:18). The divine law he delivered is reflected even now in the laws of civilized peoples, including our own.

2. *The books of History* begin with Joshua and end with Esther. These books cover a period of approximately 1,000 years, from the conquest of the promised land about 1400 BC to the end of the Old Testament about 400 BC. Naturally, they cannot tell everything that happened, but they record the course of history in a general way and show clearly the effects both of following God's law and of ignoring it. The books deal principally with the Hebrews because it was through them that the Christ was to come.

3. *The books of Poetry* are more correctly labeled Wisdom Literature. They include Job through Song of Solomon. This type of writing was a popular genre in the ancient Near East and focused on how people respond to God in worship and lifestyle. Few scholars today are familiar with much ancient poetry, but the poetry of the Bible is held and honored in millions of devout hearts. How shall we account for these facts unless we agree that Bible poetry is inspired of God?

4. *The books of Prophecy* are divided into 2 subgroups: major prophets (the first 5) and minor prophets (the latter 12). The labels "major" and "minor" refer only to the length of the books and not their importance.

We commonly use the term *prophet* today to refer solely to someone foretelling the future. But biblical prophets did much more. While the civil authority in Israel lay with the king and religious authority with the priesthood, the prophets were independent from either. Prophets spoke messages from God that would call for social reform when the nation strayed from God's plan. Prophets might tell of mystical visions, use props to proclaim their messages, or even act out their communication from God. They also predicted the near future, and some prophets clearly spoke of a future coming king—the Messiah, or Christ. Lesson 17 lists some of the prophecies that were fulfilled in Christ.

DIVISIONS OF THE NEW TESTAMENT

NEW = 3 Letters
TESTAMENT = 9 ltts
3 X 9 = 27!
Books.

Just as there are 4 kinds of books in the Old Testament, so there are 4 kinds in the New Testament: Gospels (4 books), History (1 book), Letters (21 books), Prophecy (1 book).

A. PURPOSES OF THE 4 GROUPS

In studying any passage of Scripture, it is important to know to whom it is addressed. In this we are helped by having a general idea of the purpose of each kind of book.

For example, Acts is a book of history, recording the beginning of the church and telling how people became Christians. "Repent, and be baptized" (Acts 2:38) is not addressed to Christians, but to non-Christians.

On the other hand, the letters are written to Christians to help them live as Christ would have them live. In 1 of them we read, "Pure religion and undefiled before God and the Father is this, To visit the fatherless and widows in their affliction, and to keep himself unspotted from the world" (James 1:27). This is addressed to Christians, not to non-Christians.

A non-Christian should not ignore Acts 2:38, which is addressed to him, or try to follow

James 1:27, which is not addressed to him. And a Christian should not be content because he has obeyed Acts 2:38, which was addressed to him in his former condition. He should now follow James 1:27, which is addressed to him in his present condition as a Christian.

1. *The Gospels* tell about the life, death, and resurrection of Jesus. Their purpose is to lead us to believe that He is the Christ, the Son of God. John 20:31 states this purpose.

2. *The book of History*, Acts, tells how the church began and carried on its work, and how people became Christians. Its purpose is to show people today how to become Christians and carry on the work of the church.

3. *The Letters* are addressed to Christians. Their purpose is to guide Christians in their living, helping them to do whatever Jesus commanded (see Matthew 28:20). Romans 12 is a good example of their teaching.

4. *The book of Prophecy*, Revelation, tells of the final victory of Christ and His people. It encourages us to keep on living as Christians ought to live. Its message is summed up as follows: "Be thou faithful unto death, and I will give thee a crown of life" (Revelation 2:10).

B. SOME FACTS ABOUT THE 4 GROUPS

1. *The Gospels* record a time of transition. They are properly listed as a part of the New Testament, but in the period they cover, the Old Testament law was still in effect. Jesus lived in the Jewish, or Mosaic, dispensation. He was circumcised according to the law; He worshipped in the synagogues. When a man asked Him what good thing to do to inherit eternal life, He referred to the Old Testament law. Nevertheless, He was preparing for the time of the new covenant and training His apostles to be its messengers. The new dispensation was dramatically ushered in on the Day of Pentecost, 50 days after Jesus rose from the dead.

During the period of the Gospels, Jesus was here in the flesh, walking among humankind as Lord and Master. He could and did say to a person, "Thy sins are forgiven thee"; to another, "Thy faith hath made thee whole"; to another, "Rise, take up thy bed, and walk"; and to a thief on a cross, "Today shalt thou be with me in paradise." But when His work of preparation was completed by His death and resurrection, He sent the Holy Spirit to guide His chosen apostles as they proclaimed the way of salvation for all men for all time. That way is taught in the whole New Testament.

2. *The book of History* in the New Testament is the book of Acts. It tells how the church began and grew as the apostles obeyed the Great Commission of Matthew 28:19, 20. Since the Holy Spirit guided these men, we know we are following the leading of the Holy Spirit when we teach as they taught and bring people to Christ in the same way they did.

3. *The Letters* tell Christians how they ought to live, how to do what Jesus taught. However, not all their teaching is intended for all Christians. There are instructions for new Christians, or "babes" in Christ, and there are instructions for those who have lived in Christ and should have gone far in Christian attainment. There are instructions for deacons and elders. There are instructions for widows, for parents, for children. There are instructions for servants and masters. But of course, there are many parts of the letters that do give instructions for all who are trying to follow Christ.

4. *The book of Prophecy*, Revelation, is written in a style unfamiliar to the Western mind. The genre is called apocalyptic literature, and examples of it can be found in Jewish writing beginning about the 5th century BC. Parts of other biblical books, such as Daniel 7–12 and Matthew 24:3-31, are examples of apocalypses. The word *apocalypse* means "unveiling," or "revelation." The

book of Revelation communicates through dramatic action, strange characters, and symbols (many coming from the Old Testament).

Christians are divided on how best to understand Revelation. Some see the book as dealing only with the distant future. Others see it as primarily dealing with events unfolding at the time of John in light of the future coming of Christ at the end of the age. However, the book as a whole brings a helpful and encouraging message that every Christian reader can easily grasp. It is obviously a book on faithfulness, calling us to be true to Christ regardless of all difficulties, and promising the final victory of righteousness.

MAIN IDEAS OF THIS LESSON

The Old Testament has _39_ books: 5 books of ~~History~~ LAW, 12 books of _History_, _5_ books of Poetry, and _17_ books of Prophecy.

The New Testament has _27_ books: 4 _GOSPELS_, 1 book of _HISTORY_, _21_ Letters, and 1 book of _PROPHECY_.

Biblical prophets did more than tell the _FUTURE_. They gave messages directly from God that His people needed to hear.

During the period of the Gospels, Jesus was here in the _FLESH_, walking among _HUMANKIND_ as Lord and Master.

The book of Acts tells how the church _BEGAN_ and _GREW_.

The Letters tell _CHRISTIANS_ how they ought to _LIVE_.

QUESTIONS FOR DEEPER CONSIDERATION AND DISCUSSION

1. Think of how books are organized in a library or in a bookstore. Why do we need to know how those books are organized? How is the Bible organized, and how does understanding that organization help us find information in God's library? ORGANIZED TOPICALLY/GENRE'S

2. The Old Testament focuses on the history of the Jews. Why would God focus on a single nation to the exclusion of others? How does understanding this focus help us interpret the content and commands of the Old Testament? Wanted a people group/chosen nation. Helps understand that God is faithful/unchanging & his love for us

3. It could be said that Jesus lived under the Mosaic covenant but lived to usher in a new covenant. What do you think is meant by that? Why is it important to understand? He replaced the old. Important b/c it includes ALL people & then its important b/c must understand NEW & abide by it and not the OLD. Also know that eternal life is included.

4. Why do you believe Christians find the book of Revelation hard to understand? How do the 2 ways of approaching the book contribute to that difficulty? Haven't read OT, & uses a ton of symbolism. Distant future vs unfolding presently.

BOOKS OF THE OLD TESTAMENT

The Bible is the Christian's tool chest. In Christian teaching and in winning people to Christ, no human reasoning can equal the Scriptures themselves. There is Scripture to fit every need, and the Christian should know where to find what he or she needs at a particular time. A start in this direction is to learn to name the books of the Bible in order.

——— BOOKS OF LAW ———

There are 5 books of Law: *Genesis, Exodus, Leviticus, Numbers, Deuteronomy*. These 5 books are called the Pentateuch (pronounced *Pen*-ta-teuk), from the Greek *penta* ("5") and *teuchos* ("book"). Tradition tells us that Moses wrote them. The last chapter, telling of Moses' death, was obviously added by another writer, possibly Joshua.

1. *Genesis* means "beginning." Moses needed divine guidance in order to tell of the events of creation, because they occurred when no man was present to observe and record them. God revealed to Moses what had happened. Genesis also traces briefly the history of mankind through many centuries until the children of Israel were living in Egypt about 1500 BC.

2. *Exodus* means "going out." This book tells how the people of Israel went out of Egypt and at Mount Sinai received from God the law that was to govern them as an independent nation under God.

3. *Leviticus* takes its name from the tribe of Levi, 1 of the 12 tribes of Israel. All the men of this tribe were dedicated to religious service. One family of them became priests, and the rest were assistants to the priests, musicians in the choir and orchestra, caretakers in the tabernacle or temple, and so on. The book of Leviticus contains special laws for these Levites and <u>gives specific instructions for sacrifices and worship</u>.

4. *Numbers* is so called because it tells how the people of Israel were twice numbered in national censuses. It also records part of the law not included in Exodus and tells of the wandering of Israel in the desert between Sinai and the promised land.

5. *Deuteronomy* means the "second law." After the Israelites spent 40 years in the wilderness, it was a whole new generation preparing to enter the promised land than had witnessed the giving of the law. Therefore, Moses took the opportunity to review the law and remind that adherence to God's Word would bring them safety and security in their new land.

——— BOOKS OF HISTORY ———

There are 12 books of History. For easy memorization, try grouping them as follows: *Joshua, Judges, Ruth; 1 & 2 Samuel, 1 & 2 Kings, 1 & 2 Chronicles; Ezra, Nehemiah, Esther*. These books cover about 1,000 years, from 1400 BC to 400 BC.

The first 3 books tell how Israel conquered the promised land and lived there with the judges as their leaders. Although God was to be the only king of Israel, the people became lawless because there was no civil authority on the throne.

The 3 pairs of books that follow tell how Israel became a monarchy and rose to become a great nation. Yet after the golden age of David and Solomon, the nation split—with Israel in the north and Judah in the south. Assyria conquered the rebel nation of Israel first. But Judah followed the same rebellious path and later fell to the nation of Babylon.

The final 3 books tell of events in Palestine and in Persia after the Babylonian captivity was ended. The priest Ezra restored religious order and helped supervise rebuilding the temple that the Babylonians had destroyed. Esther, an orphaned Jewish captive, providentially rose to power in Persia and saved her people from genocide. Esther was also the stepmother of Persian king Artaxerxes. Artaxerxes allowed another Jewish captive by the name of Nehemiah to go back to Judah and restore civil order for the Jews returning home.

─── BOOKS OF POETRY ───

There are 5 books of Poetry (more accurately called Wisdom Literature): *Job, Psalms, Proverbs, Ecclesiastes, Song of Solomon*. From the standpoint of age, influence, permanence, and beauty, these books are seen to tower above all the other poetry of the world.

1. *Job* is a dramatic debate in poetic form, dealing with the problem of human suffering. It brings a lesson of unfaltering trust in God. Job lived before the giving of the law of Moses, so he did not have Scripture to guide him. The book shows how he and others struggled to understand the nature of God and His justice in the absence of special revelation.

2. *Psalms* is a collection of songs, many of them by David. No doubt several of them were specially written for use in the worship in the temple.

3. *Proverbs* is a collection of short, pointed sayings. Most of them were written by Solomon.

4. *Ecclesiastes* means "the preacher." This is the name given to himself by Solomon, who wrote the book (Ecclesiastes 1:1). This book can be seen as a debate with those who claim life is meaningless. A person who separates verses from the context of the entire book might conclude that the book is dark and depressing. But be sure to read the preacher's closing argument in Ecclesiastes 12:13, 14!

5. *Song of Solomon* is an operetta, the work of Solomon. While some have tried to interpret it as a prophecy of the love between Christ and His church, the New Testament never identifies it as such. It is probably best understood as being exactly what it seems to be—a frank and joyful celebration of marital love.

─── BOOKS OF PROPHECY ───

There are 17 books of Prophecy. For easy memorizing they can be listed in 4 groups, with 5 in the first group and 4 in each of the others:

- The **major prophets** are: *Isaiah, Jeremiah, Lamentations, Ezekiel, Daniel.*
- The **minor prophets** are: *Hosea, Joel, Amos, Obadiah; Jonah, Micah, Nahum, Habakkuk; Zephaniah, Haggai, Zechariah, Malachi.*

A. MAJOR PROPHETS

The first 5 books of Prophecy are called major because they are longer, not more important, than the other books. All the major prophets were sent to the southern kingdom of Judah.

1. *Isaiah* lived in Jerusalem and prophesied during the reigns of 5 kings: Uzziah, Jotham, Ahaz, Hezekiah, and Manasseh. His book warns of the captivity that would come because of sin, and it promises restoration after the captivity. More than 700 years before Christ, Isaiah foretold the Savior so clearly that his book is sometimes called "the Gospel according to Isaiah."

2. *Jeremiah* lived in Jerusalem before and during the invasions that brought defeat and captivity. He too pointed out that captivity would come, and he promised that the nation would be restored in about 70 years. Note his promise of a new covenant in Jeremiah 31:31-34.

3. *Lamentations* was written by Jeremiah. In it he laments the fate of Jerusalem but confesses that it was a just punishment for her sins.

4. *Ezekiel*, a captive in Babylon, vividly rebukes the sins of the people and defends the justice of God. His ministry overlaps the end of Jeremiah's ministry and the beginning of Daniel's.

5. *Daniel* also was a captive, but he became a trusted adviser of the Babylonian king. His book is notable for foretelling the great empires of Persia, Greece, and Rome that would follow the empire of Babylon.

B. MINOR PROPHETS

The 12 minor prophets are placed after the major prophets in the arrangement of the Bible, but Obadiah, Joel, Jonah, and Amos actually lived and taught earlier than any of the major prophets. Only Haggai, Zechariah, and Malachi came later than any of the major prophets. These minor prophets are also distinguished by the people they were called to correct.

1. *Hosea, Amos,* and *Jonah* were commanded to call rebellious Israel to repentance. All preached within the same century. Hosea pictured God's unconditional love as the willingness of a man agreeing to be reunited with a faithless wife. Amos was a shepherd and farmer from Judah whom God used to condemn social injustice in Israel. Jonah was shown that God could even forgive the political enemies of Israel, the Assyrians. The people of Nineveh, the capital of Assyria, repented, but God's chosen in Israel did not!

2. *Joel, Obadiah, Micah, Nahum, Habakkuk,* and *Zephaniah* called the southern kingdom of Judah to repentance. Early on, Joel could see the sins that would finally lead to disaster. Obadiah briefly foretold the destruction of Edom, an enemy nation. Micah lived at the same time as Isaiah and brought a similar message. Through his book Jewish scholars knew Christ was to be born in Bethlehem (Micah 5:2; Matthew 2:1-6). After Assyria conquered Israel, Nahum promised that Nineveh would not escape judgment. As the threat of Babylonian conquest loomed, Zephaniah and Habakkuk joined Jeremiah in issuing Judah a final warning.

3. *Haggai, Zechariah,* and *Malachi* were sent to those who returned to Jerusalem after the Babylonian captivity. Haggai and Zechariah urged the people not to fall prey to fear or complacency but to complete the task of rebuilding the temple. Zechariah promised that the temple would someday welcome Zion's king, the Messiah. Malachi was the last of the Old Testament prophets. His book closes with a prophecy that was fulfilled 400 years later in John the Baptist, the forerunner of Jesus (Malachi 4:5, 6; Matthew 11:11-14).

C. THE PROPHETS AND THEIR WORK

There were many more prophets besides those whose books are found in the books of Prophecy. Elijah and Elisha are among the most famous. Some prophets, like Isaiah, were trusted counselors of kings. Some, like Amos, were ordinary men who became preachers of righteousness. Some, like Elijah and Elisha, were regarded as political dissidents. Kings of their day gladly would have killed them! But all the prophets faithfully delivered the messages God gave them to deliver. All of them were authorized spokesmen for the Almighty, whether the message had to do with sin and righteousness in their own times, with events coming in the next decades, or with the coming of Christ hundreds of years in the future.

MAIN IDEAS OF THIS LESSON

The 5 books of Law (also known as the Pentateuch) are:

GENESIS   EXODUS   LEVITICUS

NUMBERS   DEUTERONOMY

The 12 books of History are:

JOSHUA   JUDGES   RUTH

1 & 2 SAMUEL   1 & 2 ~~CHRONICLES~~ KINGS 1 & 2 CHRONICLES

EZRA   NEHEMIAH   ESTHER

The 5 books of Poetry (also known as Wisdom Literature) are:

JOB   PSALMS   PROVERBS

ECCLESIASTES   SONG OF SOLOMON

In the Prophecy books, the 5 books of major prophets (called so for their length, not importance) are:

ISAIAH   JEREMIAH   LAMENTATIONS

EZEKIAL   DANIEL

The 12 books of minor prophets (called so for their length, not importance) are:

HOSEA   AMOS   JONAH   JOEL

OBADIAH   MICAH   NAHUM   HABBAKKUK

ZEPHANIAH   HAGGAI   ZECHARIAH   MALACHI

QUESTIONS FOR DEEPER CONSIDERATION AND DISCUSSION

1. Consider the content of the books of Job, Ecclesiastes, and Song of Solomon. Why might some be surprised to find such content in the Scriptures? Why do you think these books are included?

B/c it has suffering, confessions of life being meaningless, $

2. God often sent more than 1 prophet to preach at around the same time. Using the information in this lesson and other references such as Bible handbooks and time lines, group some prophets together whose ministries overlapped. What was so important about each of those times that required sending a prophet? Why might God have sent more than 1 prophet with the same controversial messages?

BOOKS OF THE NEW TESTAMENT

—— THE GOSPELS ——

The word *gospel* means "good news." Each of these books gives the good news that Jesus came to earth, died to save us from sin and death, and rose from the dead, bringing "life and immortality to light" (2 Timothy 1:10). Because they tell of the earthly life of Jesus, the Gospels are referred to as biographies, but in fact, they focus primarily on Jesus' 3 years of ministry.

The Gospels were written by the men whose names they bear. Matthew and John were 2 of the 12 apostles, eyewitnesses of Jesus' ministry. Early Christian testimony indicates that Peter supplied most of the information given in Mark's Gospel. Luke is the only New Testament writer who probably was not Jewish. He likely spent 2 years in Palestine, collecting information from many eyewitnesses of Jesus' ministry and writing his record under the direction of the Holy Spirit.

Why are there 4 stories of the life of Christ instead of only 1? It is important to note that no written account of Jesus' life existed during the first years of the church. Unlike modern culture, the culture of the first recipients of the good news passed along carefully rehearsed accounts verbally, with astounding accuracy.

Matthew, Mark, and Luke penned their accounts between the years of AD 50–70. They all seemed to use the same general outline, most likely the same outline passed along verbally in the early church and originating from the apostles. We call these 3 books the synoptic Gospels, using a Greek word meaning that they came from the "same viewpoint." Yet each inspired writer tailored his Gospel to a specific audience and used his own style and experiences to make each unique.

Matthew seems to have been written especially for Jews who knew the Old Testament and were looking for the Messiah. Often it points out the fulfillment of prophecy (see Matthew 1:22, 23; 2:1-6, 13-15, 16-18, for example). *Mark* is a short, vigorous record such as would appeal to the active Romans. Often prompt action is indicated (Mark 1:12, 18, 20, 28, 29, 42). *Luke* is a literary masterpiece that would appeal to cultured Greeks like Luke himself.

John was written as much as 30 years after the synoptic Gospels. Instead of using the traditional outline, John structured his Gospel around 7 sign miracles that demonstrated decisively that Jesus is God's Son (see John 20:31). John also purposely recorded the many "I am" statements of Jesus, such as "I am the light of the world" (John 8:12). Those who knew the Old Testament surely recognized the words "I am" as how God identified himself to Moses in the burning bush (Exodus 3:14).

——— HISTORY ———

Acts (often titled the Acts of the Apostles) is the 1 book of History in the New Testament. Written by Luke, it is a continuation of his Gospel. Luke was a frequent companion of Paul, and he tells more of the acts of Paul than of any other apostle. Luke also includes himself when talking about events he witnessed, by using the first person. We commonly refer to these as the "we passages" (Acts 16:10-17; 20:5-15; 21:1-18; 27:1–28:16).

By telling how people became Christians under the teaching of inspired men, Acts reveals how people may become Christians today (Acts 2, 8, 9, 10, 16). It also gives helpful records of the worship and life of Christians. For example, they continued in "the apostles' doctrine and fellowship, and in breaking of bread, and in prayers" (Acts 2:42). They took care of needy Christians (6:1-6). When they were driven from home, they went everywhere preaching the word (8:4).

——— THE LETTERS ———

The New Testament has 21 books that are Letters. Some prefer the name Epistles, which means "the same." Each letter is named either for the writer or for the person or group of people to whom it was written.

A. PAUL'S LETTERS

The first 14 letters are attributed to Paul, though no one really knows who wrote the fourteenth, Hebrews. These 14 may be memorized in 4 groups—3, 4, 4, 3: *Romans* and *1 & 2 Corinthians; Galatians, Ephesians, Philippians, Colossians; 1 & 2 Thessalonians* and *1 & 2 Timothy; Titus, Philemon, Hebrews.*

B. LETTERS FROM OTHERS

The remaining 7 letters were written by 4 authors, and each is named for its writer. They are easily memorized by grouping them by author: *James, 1 & 2 Peter, 1 & 2 & 3 John, Jude.*

C. OTHER DESIGNATIONS

Paul's letters sometimes are called special letters because each is addressed to a special person, such as 1 & 2 Timothy, or to a church in a specific place, such as Romans. Galatians is addressed to several churches in a certain area. Hebrews often is included in this group for the sake of convenience, even though it has no special address.

The remaining letters are called general letters (or epistles) because they are not addressed to any particular person or group. The exceptions are 2 & 3 John, included in this group for the sake of convenience. You may also hear these letters referred to as the catholic letters/epistles. The word *catholic* in this usage is not capitalized and means "universal" rather than referring to the Roman Catholic Church.

Four of Paul's letters are called prison epistles (or captivity epistles): Ephesians, Philippians, Colossians, and Philemon. Paul wrote these while he was a prisoner, probably in Rome (Acts 28:16-31). Three of Paul's letters are called pastoral epistles: 1 & 2 Timothy, Titus. These were written to help Timothy and Titus in guiding, or shepherding, Christian people. The word *pastor* literally means "shepherd."

—— PROPHECY ——

Revelation, the 1 book of Prophecy, is an example of apocalyptic literature, a genre that does not exist in modern literature (recall our discussion of this in lesson 3). John the apostle recorded the vision Jesus gave him while he was a political prisoner on the island of Patmos. It was written during the first widespread persecution of the church shortly before AD 100. It pictures the dramatic conflict between good and evil and teaches the final victory of Christ and His people.

MAIN IDEAS OF THIS LESSON

The 4 Gospels were written by the early church leaders whose names they bear:
_____ , _____ , _____ , and _____ .

Luke, a frequent companion of _____ , wrote the book of _____ .
It tells the history and practices of the first church.

The 14 letters of Paul are: _____ , 1 & 2 _____ ,
_____ , _____ , _____ ,
_____ , 1 & 2 _____ , 1 & 2 _____ ,
_____ , _____ , and _____ .
This last letter is included in this group, but its author is not definitely known.

The 7 general letters are: _____ , 1 & 2 _____ , 1 & 2
& 3 _____ , and _____ .

The book of _____ shows the final
_____ of Christ and His people.

QUESTIONS FOR DEEPER CONSIDERATION AND DISCUSSION

1. The world in which the early church began was deeply divided culturally between Jews, the ruling Romans, and the intellectual Greeks. With that in mind, distinguish between the four Gospels and tell why those differences are important.

2. Compare and contrast the book of Acts with the founding documents of human organizations.

3. List Paul's prison epistles and his pastoral epistles. How might his situation and his audience have shaped the content of those letters?

4. John wrote the book of Revelation while he was a political prisoner and during a time when the most powerful empire in the world was threatening the church. How do you think those circumstances might have affected not only the message of the book but also the style in which it was written?

3 DISPENSATIONS

A *dispensation* is a plan, or way, by which God dispenses, or gives out, His revelation, His blessing, and His punishment. Taking a broad view of all history, we see that God has dealt with mankind according to 3 great plans. Though we will be calling them dispensations here, they are sometimes called: patriarchal age, Jewish (or Mosaic) age, and Christian (or the church) age.

—— THE PATRIARCHAL —— DISPENSATION

In the earliest ages of mankind, it is recorded that God revealed His will to some of the patriarchs. The word *patriarchs* means "chief fathers."

A. SOME OF THE PATRIARCHS

Among the chief ancestors to whom God gave revelations are Adam, Noah, and Abraham. To *Adam* God gave a home, a task, and a prohibition, along with dominion over the rest of the earthly creation (Genesis 1:28, 29; 2:15-17). To *Noah* God gave blessing and dominion and prohibitions and promise (9:1-17). To *Abraham* God gave a call, a home, and a promise (12:1-3).

B. PATRIARCHAL WORSHIP

The *altar* was the institution of worship in patriarchal times. The offering of sacrifices began at least as early as Abel (Genesis 4:3, 4). Some speculate that God demonstrated sacrifice to Adam and Eve when He made animal-skin clothing for them (3:21). In this way, God would have vividly illustrated that sacrifice was necessary as a covering for sin. Noah and Abraham also built altars and made sacrifices (8:20; 12:8), as did other patriarchs.

—— THE JEWISH (OR MOSAIC) —— DISPENSATION

A. BEGINNING OF A NEW DISPENSATION

The patriarchal dispensation ended and a new dispensation began when God gave the law, with a promise that the people would be blessed when they obeyed and punished when they disobeyed. This is called the Jewish dispensation because the Jews were the people who received the law. It is sometimes called the Mosaic dispensation because God gave the law through Moses.

B. JEWISH WORSHIP

In the Jewish dispensation, worship centered in the *tabernacle,* in which the altar of sacrifice had a prominent place. Later the tabernacle was replaced by the temple, and still later the synagogues were added. These will be studied in lessons 13 and 14.

THE CHRISTIAN (OR CHURCH) DISPENSATION

A. THE EXTENT OF THE CHRISTIAN DISPENSATION

The earthly life and work of Jesus laid the foundation for a new dispensation. His death was the long-awaited, perfect sacrifice for the forgiveness of sins. This ended the dispensation of the Mosaic law. Soon afterward the new dispensation was announced with the birth of the church on the Day of Pentecost, AD 30 (Acts 2). This age of the church will continue until the return of Jesus.

B. A DISTINCTIVE FEATURE

God now dispenses salvation and blessing by His grace—not because we deserve them. Christians do try earnestly to do the Lord's will in everything; but they know they fail, and so depend on the Lord's forgiveness.

C. CHRISTIAN WORSHIP

The *church* is the institution of worship in the Christian dispensation. God does not dwell in a building. Rather, the Holy Spirit indwells individual believers (Acts 2:38; Romans 8:9). So the church collectively (all Christians) replaces temple and tabernacle (1 Corinthians 3:16; 6:19; 1 Peter 2:5), and Christ's sacrifice of His life replaces the sin offerings made at the altar.

OTHER NAMES OF THE DISPENSATIONS

A. PROMISE, LAW, GRACE

The patriarchal dispensation is sometimes called the dispensation of promise because of the promises made to the patriarchs. The Jewish dispensation is known also as the dispensation of the law because the law was given to guide the Jews. The Christian dispensation is called the dispensation of grace because Christians rely on God's grace for their salvation.

B. STARLIGHT, MOONLIGHT, SUNLIGHT

The patriarchal dispensation is called the starlight dispensation because the only divine revelation given to lighten the world consisted of the communications to the patriarchs. The Jewish dispensation is called the moonlight dispensation because the revelation of God's law gave added light to guide mankind. The Christian dispensation is called the sunlight dispensation because the revelation given through Christ and the apostles is far more complete and brilliant than the former revelations.

MAIN IDEAS OF THIS LESSON

In the course of history, we see that God has dealt with humankind according to 3 great plans called _____.

In the earliest days of humankind, God dealt with people through individual family heads called _____.

The _____ dispensation is also called the _____ dispensation because the law of Moses is central to it.

The _____ dispensation began with the birth of the _____ on the Day of _____ in AD 30.

QUESTIONS FOR DEEPER CONSIDERATION AND DISCUSSION

1. We have given each dispensation 3 separate labels. What is the significance of each?

2. The disruption in the relationship between humankind and God due to the fall of mankind (Genesis 3) had to be corrected. Why do you think God did this in 3 steps (dispensations) rather than just 1? How does each dispensation build on the preceding dispensation?

3. Some religious groups such as Islam and the Church of Jesus Christ of Latter-Day Saints (Mormonism) say that God gave revelation after the New Testament that shows a "more complete" path to God. How would you answer that idea?

A TIME LINE OF BIBLE HISTORY

THE OLD TESTAMENT WORLD

Fairy tales and myths take place "once upon a time in a land far, far away." The Bible accounts, in stark contrast, took place at specific times in history in places we can locate on a map! The history and geography of the Scriptures are another testimony to its truthfulness.

—— GEOGRAPHICAL FEATURES ——

A. LAND AREAS

Three areas are most important in Old Testament history: *Mesopotamia, Canaan,* and *Egypt.* Note that the area between Mesopotamia and Canaan is desert. Therefore, the usual route between the 2 areas was to travel from northern Mesopotamia to Syria and then south into Canaan.

Egypt and Canaan were also separated by a desert area known as the *Sinai Peninsula.* A normal route between the countries would be to follow the coast of the Mediterranean Sea. When escaping from Egypt, the Israelites took a southern route, following the northern coasts of the Red Sea.

B. BODIES OF WATER

Four rivers are prominent in the Old Testament: *Tigris, Euphrates, Nile,* and *Jordan.* The Tigris and Euphrates are the freshwater sources that nourish Mesopotamia. The Nile flows through Africa and is the major waterway of Egypt. The Jordan is the major river of Canaan and flows between the Dead Sea in the south and the Sea of Galilee in the north. In the Old Testament, the Dead Sea was called the salt sea (Genesis 14:3), and the Sea of Galilee was known as the sea of Chinnereth, or Kinnereth (Numbers 34:11).

Three larger bodies of water are also a part of the Old Testament landscape: *Persian Gulf, Red Sea,* and *Mediterranean Sea.* The Persian Gulf is not directly mentioned in the Old Testament, but the Tigris and Euphrates empty into this body of water. The Red Sea separates Egypt from the Arabian Peninsula. The Israelites crossed a northern arm of this sea as they left Egypt. The Mediterranean Sea was called the great sea in Old Testament days (Joshua 1:4). The prophet Jonah would have been crossing this sea as he was trying to flee from God (Jonah 1:3).

C. MOUNTAINS

While there are many mountains in this area of the world, 3 play important roles in Old Testament history: *Mount Sinai, Mount Nebo,* and *Mount Carmel.* Sinai, where the law was given to Israel, is in the southern part of the Sinai Peninsula (Exodus 19). Nebo overlooks Canaan on the eastern shore of the Dead Sea. Moses was allowed to see the promised land from this mountain before he died (Deuteronomy 34). One of the most famous contests in the Bible took place on Mount Carmel in northern Canaan near the Mediterranean Sea. It was there Elijah challenged the prophets of Baal (1 Kings 18:16-46).

——— HISTORICAL HIGHLIGHTS ———

Old Testament history traces the accounts of 5 great empires: *Egypt, Israel, the Assyrian Empire, the Babylonian Empire,* and *the Medo-Persian Empire.*

Egypt has a history as a powerful African nation with several great dynasties. The people of Israel were guests there and were later enslaved (Exodus 1:1-10). After entering the promised land, Israel became a world power under Solomon. Solomon extended his empire from the border of Egypt to the Euphrates (2 Chronicles 8:1-6). After the time of Solomon, the kings of Judah tried to maintain peace by forging alliances with Egypt to balance the power of the emerging Assyrian Empire in Mesopotamia (2 Kings 18:21).

After the golden age of Solomon, 3 great empires arose in Mesopotamia. Assyria conquered all of Mesopotamia, much of Egypt, and the rebellious northern kingdom of Israel (2 Kings 17). Nineveh was its capital. Then Babylonia conquered Assyria and took all its territory. Under King Nebuchadnezzar, Babylon destroyed Jerusalem and took most of the remaining Jews to Mesopotamia in captivity. Later, Media and Persia combined to take all this territory from Babylonia. They released the Jews from captivity but continued to rule till the close of Old Testament history (Ezra 1).

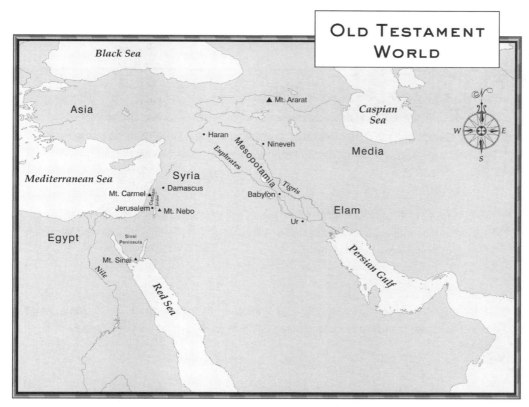

Adapted from *Standard Bible Atlas,* © Standard Publishing.

SPECIAL PLACES AND EVENTS

Some events and places especially important in biblical history are not as well documented in secular history—but that is not unexpected. Nevertheless, the Bible pinpoints their specific geographical locations, something that we would not expect if these events and places were mythological.

The Bible tells us that 4 rivers watered the Garden of Eden. Two of those were the Tigris (also called the Hiddekel) and Euphrates (Genesis 2:10-14). Furthermore, we are told the general location in which Noah's ark came to rest (8:4). The tower of Babel (or Babylon) was built where Babylon arose, in what is modern Iraq (Genesis 11).

MAIN IDEAS OF THIS LESSON

The 3 major land areas in Old Testament history are _____, _____, and _____.

The 4 major rivers in Old Testament geography are

_____, _____, _____, and _____.

The 3 major seas mentioned in the Old Testament are the _____ Sea, the _____ sea (that we call the Mediterranean Sea), and the sea of _____ (that we call the Sea of Galilee).

The 5 empires described in the Old Testament are _____, _____, _____, _____, and the _____ - _____ Empire.

QUESTIONS FOR DEEPER CONSIDERATION AND DISCUSSION

1. Fairy tales take place in unspecified lands at unspecified times. Explain how biblical references to geography and history show that the Old Testament is written as history, not mythology.

2. As 21st-century citizens of the western hemisphere, we are more familiar with our own history and geography than with any other. Why do you think knowledge of Old Testament history and geography can aid us in understanding the Bible?

3. The lands of the Old Testament are still in the news today! Try to show where modern places like the city of Cairo and the nations of Iraq and Iran would lie on the map of the Old Testament world on page 33.

OLD TESTAMENT PEOPLE—PART 1

Why study Old Testament history, since the old covenant has been replaced by the new? Old Testament history helps us understand God and the way of righteousness and provides background for the New Testament. New Testament writers often refer to Old Testament characters and events. Knowledge of these enriches our knowledge of the New Testament.

In lessons 8 and 9, you will be introduced to 16 Bible people. This will help you outline the history of the Old Testament. By the end of these lessons, attempt to have memorized their names and their places in Old Testament history and geography.

—— PEOPLE, EVENTS, AND PLACES ——

1. ADAM AND THE CREATION

When we think of the beginning of the world, we think of Adam—along with mankind, sin, and punishment. But with punishment came the first promise of a Savior who would crush the serpent, Satan (Genesis 3:15; Romans 16:20). Associated with Adam are his wife *Eve* and his sons *Cain, Abel,* and *Seth.* Adam began the patriarchal dispensation.

2. NOAH AND THE FLOOD

The first sin was by no means the last. The world was soon filled with people who, like Adam and Eve, wanted to be their own gods. Before these renegade humans destroyed the world and themselves, God intervened. Noah was willing to follow God's commands, and in the ark he and his family were saved from the great flood. Associated with Noah are his 3 sons *Shem, Ham,* and *Japheth.* To this day we call the people of the Middle East Semites, ancestors of Shem.

3. ABRAHAM AND THE CHOSEN NATION

As mankind multiplied after the flood, God began the next part of His plan to restore humankind to himself. God chose Abraham and his wife, Sarah, a couple unable to have children, to be the ancestors of a nation He would create and rule. This nation began with a miraculous birth and would witness an even greater miracle centuries later when a descendant of Abraham, Jesus of Nazareth, was born! With Abraham and Sarah we associate his nephew *Lot,* their son *Isaac,* and their grandson *Jacob,* whose name was changed to *Israel.* The 12 sons of Jacob became heads of the tribes of the nation of Israel.

4. JOSEPH AND EGYPT

Joseph was 1 of Jacob's 12 sons. Sold as a slave by his envious brothers, Joseph became a ruler in Egypt and was able to save his father and brothers from starvation and settle them comfortably in Egypt. In later times, however, their descendants were oppressed and enslaved in Egypt. With Joseph we associate his brothers *Judah* (the ancestor of Israel's kings) and *Levi* (the ancestor of Jewish priests). We also meet a *Pharaoh*, the title given to Egyptian rulers.

5. MOSES AND THE LAW

Moses was a Hebrew of the tribe of Levi, reared and trained in the palaces of a Pharaoh who held the rest of the Hebrews in slavery. God chose Moses to lead the descendants of Jacob from Egypt back to Canaan, to give them God's law, and to write the first 5 books of the Bible. With Moses we associate *Pharaoh* (not Pharaoh of Joseph's time but a later ruler who was an enemy rather than a friend); Moses' brother *Aaron,* who became the first high priest of Israel; and Moses' father-in-law, *Jethro*, a wise adviser. Moses began the Jewish dispensation.

6. JOSHUA AND THE PROMISED LAND

God had a purpose for taking the nation of Israel out of Canaan to spend 4 centuries as slaves in Egypt. He allowed the people of Canaan that time to turn from their brutal, godless ways. Yet they did not. After the death of Moses, Joshua led Israel in a God-ordained war of judgment as they wrested the land from the heathen for their home. With Joshua may be remembered *Caleb,* a faithful fellow soldier. Also notable is a Canaanite prostitute, *Rahab,* who was the only person in that land willing to repent and follow the God of Israel!

7. GIDEON AND THE JUDGES

After Joshua died, the chosen people often fell into sin and were punished by invasions of heathen people. Each time they repented of their sins, God gave a leader to help them drive out the invaders. These leaders were called judges. Gideon was among the most notable of them. We may also remember *Samson,* the strong man; *Deborah*, the woman judge; and *Ruth*, a foreign woman who became the great-grandmother of King David and an ancestor of the Messiah.

8. SAMUEL AND ISRAEL'S KINGS

Samuel was the last of the judges. He anointed the first 2 kings of Israel, Saul and David. With Samuel we may remember *Hannah*, his mother; *Eli*, the high priest who trained him; and *Joel* and *Abiah (*or *Abijah)*, his wicked sons.

MAIN IDEAS OF THIS LESSON

The first half of Old Testament history can be outlined by remembering 8 main characters and their situations:

_____ and creation, _____ and the flood, _____ and the chosen nation, _____ and a time in Egypt, _____ and the law, _____ and the conquest of the promised land, _____ and the other judges, and _____ and Israel's first kings.

1. Review the dispensations presented in lesson 6 and place each of these 8 characters in the proper dispensation.

2. Using the map on page 33, point out the area or areas associated with each of these 8 characters.

3. Some mistakenly argue that the God of the Old Testament was a God of judgment while the God of the New Testament is a God of salvation. Looking at the judgment stories of the flood and the conquest of Canaan, tell how they are actually stories of a God wanting to save.

OLD TESTAMENT CHARACTERS–I

Character	Other Characters	Place	Event	Dispensation
ADAM	Eve, Cain, Abel, Seth	Mesopotamia	Creation, Sin	Patriarchal
NOAH	Ham, Shem, Japheth	Mesopotamia	Flood	Patriarchal
ABRAHAM	Lot, Isaac, Jacob	Mesopotamia	Promise of a Nation	Patriarchal
JOSEPH	Judah, Levi, Pharaoh	Egypt	Slavery to Power to Slavery	Patriarchal
MOSES	Pharaoh, Aaron, Jethro	Egypt, Sinai	Exodus, Wilderness Wandering	Jewish
JOSHUA	Caleb, Rahab	Sinai, Canaan	Entering Promised Land	Jewish
GIDEON	Samson, Deborah, Ruth	Canaan	Period of the Judges	Jewish
SAMUEL	Hannah, Eli, Joel, Abiah (or Abijah)	Canaan	Anointing of Saul and David	Jewish

OLD TESTAMENT PEOPLE—PART 2

Lesson 8 outlined the first part of Old Testament history with 8 important people and some events and other persons associated with them. This lesson continues with the remainder of Old Testament history and 8 more characters.

—— PEOPLE, EVENTS, AND PLACES ——

9. SAUL, THE FIRST KING

In Samuel's old age, the people asked for a king. God and Samuel did not approve, but they consented. The chosen king was Saul, who proved to be an able leader for a time and won some notable victories. But all too soon he began to ignore God's will and follow his own selfish inclinations. In time this led to his defeat and death. With Saul we remember his son *Jonathan*, who was a close friend of David, and *Abner*, Saul's great general.

10. DAVID, THE GREAT KING

David was the second king of Israel. He continued the war of judgment begun by Joshua and made Israel the most powerful empire of the time. He was also a great musician and the author of many of the psalms. Though notable sins are recorded against him, the main course of his life was so good that he is known as a man after God's own heart. With David we may remember *Goliath*, the Philistine giant; *Nathan*, the prophet who confronted him because of his affair with *Bathsheba*; and *Absalom*, his conceited son who led an armed rebellion against him.

11. SOLOMON, THE WISE KING

Solomon, David's son and the next king, was especially gifted with wisdom and wrote Proverbs, Ecclesiastes, and the Song of Solomon. Trusting God, he built a magnificent temple and added glory to the great empire David had built. But then he decided to trust in more political solutions. He taxed the people too heavily and drafted them mercilessly for public works as well as for the army. He also married many women of other nations, probably as a strategy to bring peace. But these marriages introduced idolatry and wickedness into Israel. Because of his oppression and growing sin, his people were ready to revolt at the end of his reign. With Solomon we may recall the *Queen of Sheba*; Solomon's son *Rehoboam*, who became the next king; and *Jeroboam*, king of the northern part of Israel that rebelled and became an independent nation.

12. ELIJAH, THE GREAT PROPHET

After the kingdom was divided, each section had many kings, but not many *good* kings. Great prophets arose to call the civil authorities back to God. One of the greatest prophets was Elijah, who boldly stood against King Ahab and Queen Jezebel's efforts to turn the worship of Israel from the God of Israel to Baal. With Elijah we associate *Jezebel*, the heathen queen; *Ahab*, the king who brought her from Phoenicia to be his wife; and *Elisha*, another prophet who was a helper and successor of Elijah.

13. ISAIAH, THE GOSPEL PROPHET

About 700 years after Moses and 700 years before Christ, Isaiah prophesied. The northern kingdom was taken into captivity, and Assyria threatened Judah. Isaiah spoke to those times but also spoke of a servant king, the Messiah, who would come in the future. With Isaiah we remember *Sennacherib*, the Assyrian king who tried to destroy the southern kingdom; *Hezekiah*, the good king of the southern kingdom who survived the attack of Sennacherib and for a time almost ended idolatry in the south; and *Manasseh,* the wicked son and successor of Hezekiah.

14. JEREMIAH, THE WEEPING PROPHET

Jeremiah lived when Jerusalem was destroyed and the remnant of the southern kingdom was taken into captivity. He foretold and lamented the captivity, but foretold also the later restoration and the new covenant. With Jeremiah we may remember *Huldah*, the prophetess who also foretold the fall of Jersualem; *Jehoiakim*, the wicked king who burned God's Word written by Jeremiah; and *Zedekiah,* the last king of the southern kingdom.

15. DANIEL, THE BRAVE

While Jeremiah remained in the southern kingdom of Judah, Daniel was among the Israelites taken to Babylon in captivity. With God's help, he became a trusted adviser to kings of Babylon and Persia. His book also tells of great events to come, by using the apocalyptic style later used in the book of Revelation. With Daniel we associate *Nebuchadnezzar*, the Babylonian king who conquered the Old Testament world and made captives of the people of Judah; *Belshazzar*, the last Babylonian ruler of Babylon, whose doom Daniel foretold; and *Cyrus,* the Persian king who conquered Babylon and freed the Israelite captives.

16. NEHEMIAH, THE RESTORER

Nehemiah was a governor of the Jews after they returned from captivity in Babylon. He rebuilt the walls of Jerusalem, reorganized its government, and restored respect for the law of God. Associated with Nehemiah are *Artaxerxes*, the Persian king who appointed Nehemiah as governor of Judah; *Ezra*, a priest and scholar devoted to the teaching of God's law; and *Malachi*, who wrote the last Old Testament book about 400 BC.

MAIN IDEAS OF THIS LESSON

The last half of Old Testament history can be outlined by remembering 8 main characters and their characteristics:

_____, the first king; _____,
the king with God's shepherding heart; _____, the wise king;
_____ the great prophet; _____, the
gospel prophet; _____, the weeping prophet; _____,
the brave captive prophet; and _____, restorer of civil government to Israel.

QUESTIONS FOR DEEPER CONSIDERATION AND DISCUSSION

1. God was the true king of Israel, but the temporary power of the throne caused human kings to forget this. Looking at the reigns of Saul, David, and Solomon, give instances in which they each seemed to forget God's role as true ruler of His nation.

2. The book of Judges concluded that without a human king in Israel, near anarchy was the result (Judges 21:25). Solomon wrote that without prophetic visions from God, there are similar results (Proverbs 29:18). What evidence do you see in more recent history and in current events that both civil order and moral authority are necessary for a nation to survive?

OLD TESTAMENT CHARACTERS–2

Character	Other Characters	Place	Identifying Characteristic	Dispensation
SAUL	Jonathan, Abner	Canaan	First King	Jewish
DAVID	Goliath, Bathsheba, Nathan, Absalom	Jerusalem	Great King	Jewish
SOLOMON	Queen of Sheba, Rehoboam, Jeroboam	Jerusalem	Wise King	Jewish
ELIJAH	Jezebel, Ahab, Elisha	Israel	Great Prophet	Jewish
ISAIAH	Sennacherib, Hezekiah, Manasseh	Israel	Gospel Prophet	Jewish
JEREMIAH	Huldah, Jehoiakim, Zedekiah	Judah	Weeping Prophet	Jewish
DANIEL	Nebuchadnezzar, Belshazzar, Cyrus	Babylon	Brave Prophet	Jewish
NEHEMIAH	Artaxerxes, Ezra, Malachi	Jerusalem	Restorer of Civil Order	Jewish

OLD TESTAMENT PERIODS—PART 1

Old Testament history can also be outlined in 6 natural periods: probation, preparation, conquest, power, decline, and servitude. This lesson deals with the first 2 of these periods.

—— PERIOD OF PROBATION ——

Probation means "testing." In this early period man was tested to see whether he would trust God or not. Most of humankind placed their faith in themselves, preferring to be their own gods. Noah, in contrast, responded to God in faith and received His undeserved favor, or grace (Genesis 6:8). The period of probation extends from Adam to Noah, from the creation to the flood. It is recorded in Genesis 1–9.

When given the simple choice to have everything and be God's or have nothing and be their own gods, Adam and Eve made the wrong choice.

1. *The fall*—The fall of humankind brought sin into the world (Genesis 3), fundamentally altering our relationship to God.

2. *The promise of redemption*—But while humans rejected God, He did not reciprocate. God offered the promise of redemption, the pledge that He would pay an unimaginable price to restore what humankind destroyed (v. 15).

3. *The flood*—The mess Adam and Eve made only got worse as the world population grew. When God was rejected, any attempt at goodness was also discarded. God cleansed the world with a deluge, or flood. God allowed a way to escape destruction, but in the end only Noah and his family entered the ark, the vessel of grace that kept them safe (Genesis 7:11-13).

—— PERIOD OF PREPARATION ——

As people became more numerous after the flood, sin again increased. This time God did not destroy mankind but began the preparation of a special nation that would be His own, ambassadors from God to the rest of the world. The period of preparation extends from Noah to Moses, from the flood to the exodus from Egypt. It is recorded in Genesis 10–50.

1. *The dispersion*—Humankind's desire to be equals with God continued. As their numbers grew they tried to build the tower of Babel, a temple tower that would reach to Heaven. This brought about the dispersion. God dispersed (scattered) the people, separating them into tribes with different languages (Genesis 11:1-9).

2. *Journeys of the patriarchs*—The dispersed tribes became nations and even empires. But instead of choosing an established nation, God created His own—starting with an infertile couple, Abram and Sarai (later renamed Abraham and Sarah). Trusting in God, the couple along with Lot moved from Ur in Mesopotamia to Canaan (Genesis 11:31–12:5). God

miraculously gave them a son named Isaac. In the time of Isaac's son Jacob, God's new nation moved to Egypt (Genesis 45:1–46:7). Jacob's son Joseph had risen to power there.

3. *Experiences in Egypt*—At first the chosen people were honored guests in Egypt (Genesis 47:1-12), but after a change in the government, they became mistreated slaves (Exodus 1). In the centuries in Egypt, the family of 70 increased to a nation of possibly 3 million.

MAIN IDEAS OF THIS LESSON

The first period of Old Testament history can be remembered as a time of _____, or testing. This period included separation from God called the _____, as well as the _____, or flood.

The second period can be remembered as a time of _____. The _____, or scattering, occurred when humankind tried to reunite with God through their own efforts by building the _____ of _____. Because of this scattering, humankind became divided into tribes, each speaking distinct languages.

During this period, God called _____ and his family from Mesopotamia and promised to give him descendants who would become God's special nation. Before they were established as a nation in Canaan, they would spend 400 years in the nation of _____.

QUESTIONS FOR REVIEW

1. We do not have any Bible books in the handwriting of the original writers. But what 2 types of ancient documents help us be sure that the Bible of today is essentially the same as the original writings? (lesson 1).

2. Give some simple rules to follow in Bible study (lesson 2).

3. Without writing them, name the divisions of Old and New Testaments and name the books in each (lessons 3, 4, 5).

4. Name the 3 great dispensations, giving at least 2 names of each (lesson 6).

OLD TESTAMENT PERIODS—PART 2

Lesson 10 suggested this outline of Old Testament history: probation, preparation, conquest, power, decline, and servitude. This lesson deals with the middle 2 periods.

——— PERIOD OF CONQUEST ———

By the power of God, His people broke away from Egypt, crossed the desert, and conquered Canaan. The period of conquest extends from Moses to Samuel, from the exodus to the end of the judges' time. It is recorded in the Old Testament books from Exodus to 1 Samuel and contains key events and people.

1. *Lessons of Egypt*—Polytheistic cultures worship gods who each have control over certain areas of the natural world. Quite often, the head of state is viewed as 1 of these gods. We err if we see the plagues of Egypt simply as God punishing the Egyptians in 10 creative ways. Pharaoh, by refusing to free the people of God, was claiming that the gods of Egypt were superior to the God of Israel. Each plague was a contest against 1 particular god of Egypt (the god of the Nile, the god of the earth, the god of the sun . . .), culminating with a personal attack on Pharaoh and the firstborn children of all Egypt. The plagues teach not only that there is 1—and only 1—God but also that He is superior to all challengers.

2. *Experiences in the wilderness*—After 10 plagues, the people of Israel crossed the Red Sea into the wilderness. There they received the law from God through Moses and built the tabernacle as God commanded, acknowledging His power and presence with them. But when they were commanded to conquer the promised land, they acted as if success were dependent on them alone! As a result, Israel spent 40 years in the wilderness, until God raised up a new generation who would trust in His power alone (Numbers 14:20-35).

3. *Conquest of Canaan*—God gave the people of Canaan 400 years to repent while Israel was in Egypt. But these nations only became more inhumanly evil. At God's command, Joshua led Israel in executing God's judgment. The book of Joshua also records that Israel failed to complete that task as God had ordered, and pagan people remaining in the land troubled them often in later centuries.

4. *Rule of the judges*—Because He gave the law, God was the only king of Israel. Tribal leaders were to enforce that law, but did that so inconsistently that the nation disintegrated to the point of near anarchy (Judges 17:6). During this period, the disobedience of the people led to harassment and even enslavement by pagan nations. God would send His deputies that we call judges to rescue His people from the consequences of their actions. Fifteen such leaders, including Gideon, who was among the most prominent of them, are mentioned in the book of Judges. The last judge was Samuel, whose work is described in 1 Samuel.

PERIOD OF POWER

Samuel appointed the first 2 kings of Israel, Saul and David. Under the rule of Saul, David, and Solomon, Israel developed a strong central government and became the most powerful nation of the time. The period of power reached from Samuel to Solomon, from the crowning of Saul to the division of the nation after the death of Solomon. It is recorded in 1 & 2 Samuel and 1 Kings 1–11 and includes these events:

1. *Saul's rise and fall*—Saul forgot that he was occupying a throne that really belonged to God. Because of Saul's arrogance, God removed His backing from Saul and gave His favor to David. This resulted in Saul's desperate grasping at power for 15 years. When Saul died in battle against the Philistines, David took the throne (1 Samuel 31–2 Samuel 5).

2. *David's kingdom and his capital city*—Under the rule of David, Israel's borders were expanded. David established the capital of Israel in Jerusalem, and he placed the sacred ark of the covenant there (2 Samuel 5:1-10; 6:12-19).

3. *Solomon's temple and his prosperous kingdom*—After the death of David, his son Solomon ascended to the throne, ruling an empire reaching from the borders of Egypt to the Euphrates. Solomon's reign was marked with peace and prosperity. Solomon commissioned the building of the temple in Jerusalem to replace the tabernacle as the home of the ark and the center of Israel's worship (1 Kings 6).

MAIN IDEAS OF THIS LESSON

The third period of Old Testament history can be remembered as a time of _____.
This period included the plagues against the gods of _____, 40 years
in the _____, conquest of _____,
and the period of rule by the _____.

The fourth period can be remembered as a time of _____. The
first 3 kings of Israel—_____, _____, and
_____—built Israel into a powerful empire.

QUESTIONS FOR DEEPER CONSIDERATION AND DISCUSSION

1. Review the 4 periods of Old Testament history covered thus far. Name them and tell about the major events and people in each.

2. Adam and Eve wanted God's blessings but also wanted His authority for themselves. How did Pharaoh repeat that same sin? How did the people of Israel in the wilderness and during the period of the judges and, later, King Saul do likewise? What was the inevitable result?

OLD TESTAMENT PERIODS—PART 3

Lessons 10 and 11 introduced this outline of Old Testament history: probation, preparation, conquest, power, decline, and servitude. This lesson deals with the final 2 periods.

—— PERIOD OF DECLINE ——

In Solomon's time the empire of Israel was at the height of its glory. To maintain that glory Solomon taxed his people heavily and drafted workers as well as soldiers. At Solomon's death, 10 of the 12 tribes revolted against continued oppression. The split kingdom swiftly lost its power. The period of decline extended from Solomon's death to Daniel, from the division of the kingdom to the captivity in Babylon. It is recorded in 1 Kings 12–2 Kings 25 and 2 Chronicles 10–36. This period includes these key events and people:

1. *Division of the kingdom*—After the death of Solomon, his son succeeded him. Jeroboam, a trusted labor secretary for Solomon, led the 10 northern tribes to secede from the rest of the nation around 930 BC. Although the northern kingdom (also referred to as Israel, Ephraim, or Samaria) had 10 tribes to only 2 in the southern kingdom of Judah, they lacked something vital, the temple in Jerusalem. Therefore, Jeroboam built 2 temples in Israel (in Bethel and Dan) and created a parallel priesthood. That did not please God!

2. *End of the northern kingdom*—This kingdom was doomed from the beginning because it rejected the presence of God. Prophets, including Elijah, called Israel to repentance. But they refused to hear. The Assyrians overran Israel around 721 BC and took its people captive.

3. *Fall of the southern kingdom*—Even with the temple there, Judah failed to obey God. Prophets, including Isaiah and Jeremiah, warned of coming judgment, but their calls went unheeded. The Babylonians destroyed Jerusalem and took its people to Mesopotamia about 586 BC.

—— PERIOD OF SERVITUDE ——

Most of the surviving Jews were taken to Babylon as captives after Jerusalem was destroyed about 586 BC. When the Persians conquered Babylon, they allowed the Jews to return to Jerusalem about 536 BC. Though some self-government was allowed, the Jews still were subjects of the Persian Empire, and so remained till the end of Old Testament history.

For convenience, the 400 years between the Testaments are also included in this period of servitude. During most but not all those years, the Jews were subject to foreign rulers. Thus the period of servitude is reckoned from Daniel to Christ, from the destruction of Jerusalem to the beginning of New Testament history. (A more detailed description of the time between the Testaments is found on page 48.) Here are the 7 epochs of the period of servitude:

1. *Babylonian rule*—The Babylonians were also called Chaldeans. They held the Jews in the Babylonian captivity from 586 BC, until their empire was taken over by the Persians about 538 BC. Daniel read the famous writing on the wall and predicted the fall of Babylon the night before it occurred (Daniel 5).

2. *Persian rule*—The Persians allowed the captive Jews to return to Jerusalem and govern themselves, but still kept them and their land as a part of the Persian Empire. The priest Ezra returned to supervise the rebuilding of the temple and to supervise the priesthood. Nehemiah returned to restore civil order and serve as governor. Persian rule was in force at the end of the Old Testament about 400 BC. It continued till Alexander the Great overthrew the Persian Empire about 332 BC. It was during Persian rule that Malachi called the Jews to repentance and predicted that later a new prophet Elijah would introduce a new era, the day of the Lord.

3. *Greek rule*—As a part of the Greek Empire of Alexander, the Jews were treated with kindness and consideration. But Alexander died about 323 BC, and then a time of trouble began.

4. *Egyptian rule*—When Alexander died, his empire was divided among his generals, with frequent warfare between various parts. Rulers of Egypt and those of Syria fought bitterly for control of Canaan, or Palestine, the home of the Jews. For a time the Egyptians prevailed, ruling the Jews from about 323 to 204 BC.

5. *Syrian rule*—The Syrians took Palestine from the Egyptians and remained in control from about 204 to 167 BC. This was the darkest part of the Jews' servitude. With a bloody massacre, Antiochus of Syria tried to compel them to give up their faith and accept the pagan religion of the Greeks.

6. *Maccabean freedom*—Goaded to desperation by Antiochus, the Jews launched a desperate revolt. Led by Judas Maccabeus, they won their independence. This freedom was maintained from 167 to 63 BC.

7. *Roman rule*—Successors of Judas Maccabeus lost their religious zeal and became selfish politicians, battling among themselves for the rule of Palestine. Different factions sought support from Rome, which then was rising swiftly in power. In 63 BC, Pompey moved into Jerusalem, and the Jews came under Roman rule, which continued into New Testament times. Jesus was born during the reign of Herod, whom the Roman emperor appointed as king of the Jews. By the calendar we now use, the birth of Jesus was about 6–4 BC.

MAIN IDEAS OF THIS LESSON

The fifth period of Old Testament history can be remembered as a time of
_____. This period included the rebellion of the _____ northern
tribes from the _____ southern tribes, the fall of the northern kingdom to
_____, and the fall of the southern kingdom to
_____.

During the sixth period, a time of _____, God's people were
ruled by other nations. The first 5 of these, in order, are: _____
rule, _____rule, _____rule,
_____rule, and _____rule. This
was followed by a rebellion led by Judas _____ that resulted
in a period of freedom. But in 63 BC, General Pompey conquered the nation, leading to
_____ rule.

1. Name the final 2 periods of Old Testament history and tell about the major events and people in each.

2. Modern political thought rarely discusses the importance of religion in creating a stable nation. In contrast, how does Old Testament history show that obedience to God was directly related to the stability and prosperity of Israel?

OLD TESTAMENT PERIODS, EVENTS, AND SIGNIFICANT PERSONS

Period	Events	Significant Persons
Period of Probation	The Fall The Promise of Redemption The Flood (Deluge)	Adam, coming "seed of the woman," Noah
Period of Preparation	The Dispersion (Scattering) Journeys of the Patriarchs Experiences in Egypt	Abraham, Isaac, Jacob, Joseph
Period of Conquest	Lessons of Egypt Experiences in the Wilderness Conquest of Canaan Rule of the Judges	Moses, Joshua, Gideon, Samuel
Period of Power	Saul's Rise and Fall David's Kingdom and His Capital City Solomon's Temple and His Prosperous Kingdom	Saul, David, Solomon
Period of Decline	Division of the Kingdom End of the Northern Kingdom Fall of the Southern Kingdom	Elijah, Isaiah, Jeremiah
Period of Servitude	Babylonian Rule Persian Rule Greek Rule Egyptian Rule Syrian Rule Maccabean Freedom Roman Rule	Daniel, Nehemiah, Ezra, Malachi

BETWEEN THE TESTAMENTS

The Old Testament canon closed with the restoration of the Jews to their homeland under the direction of Cyrus of Persia. They returned with high expectations for the golden age of Israel to be restored. But the years came and went to be met only with hardship, deprivation, and difficulty. Three significant tasks were completed—restoring the temple, rebuilding the city walls, reestablishing the law community—but the restoration of old Israel was not to be realized.

The nearly 400 years between the Testaments was not all peace and quiet, merely waiting for the coming of Jesus. Neither was it a time of unprecedented fidelity to the law of God. Rather, it was another of those periods of tension with the surrounding culture and subsequent compromise with the pagan forces that preyed on them.

——— RISE OF ALEXANDER ———

Persia dominated the world until 334 BC. The Persian Empire extended over what is now Iraq, Iran, Lebanon, Israel, Jordan, Egypt, Turkey, parts of Greece, the Balkans, Russia, Afghanistan, and Pakistan. But those in the West weren't content for Persian control to continue. And Alexander of Macedon proposed to do something about it.

Young Alexander had studied under Aristotle, who was an expert in the study of political institutions. Aristotle had once said, "The Greeks might govern the world, could they combine into one political society." That possibility became Alexander's dream. In 4 short years, by 330 BC, he had captured the world and reportedly wept because there was no more to conquer.

Alexander the Great died in 323 BC, and the kingdom went to an unborn son. Practically, however, it was divided into 4 areas under 4 generals. These 2 are of particular interest:

Seleucus provided oversight to Mesopotamia and Syria. The center was at Antioch. *Ptolemy* ruled Egypt, and the center was at Alexandria. An intense power struggle ensued, and Palestine was caught in the middle as usual. Late in the 4th century BC, Palestine fell to the Ptolemies, who ruled for 100 years. The Ptolemies permitted their subjects a great deal of autonomy. Although Hellenization was a part of their program, it was not pursued vigorously. The Jews were permitted to practice their unique religion. (Even so, the priesthood was far from pure.)

——— RISE OF THE SELEUCIDS ———

In 198 BC, Antiochus III, a Seleucid, claimed Palestine and crushed the Ptolemies. In many ways he inherited a unified world, at least from a surface view. Oriental civilizations had destroyed themselves. The Jews had begun to speak Greek. (The Old Testament was even translated into Greek in the mid-200s BC. It was called the Septuagint.) In 175 BC, Antiochus Epiphanes ascended the throne. This brought uneasy matters to a head, for he began an aggressive Hellenizing campaign and imposed heavy taxation.

The collision course was hastened when this Antiochus proclaimed himself the *epiphanes* ("visible incarnation") of Zeus and demanded worship. That was too much for faithful Jews. He also sold the high priesthood to Jason who was the highest bidder. The Jews were repressed.

In 168 BC, Antiochus Epiphanes marched on Jerusalem. He took the city and celebrated by offering swine's flesh on the altar of the temple and suspending the practice of Judaism. He forbade observance of the Sabbath and circumcision. Many Jews capitulated, but others didn't—and were severely mistreated.

RISE OF THE MACCABEES

Mattathias was a Jew who refused to capitulate to Antiochus's demands. He and his sons were able to lead a revolt by which temple worship was restored. Mattathias died very soon. His son Judas Maccabeus (the Hammer) caused Antiochus to back off and defeated several regional powers. Over a 3-year period he brought a semblance of peace. He was of the Hasmonean House from which came the high priests for many years thereafter. But the high priests became corrupt and accommodated heathen practices. The book of 1 Maccabees reports the wars and problems of the period. Religious motivations were frequently secondary.

RISE OF ROME

In 63 BC, Palestine fell to Roman rule when Pompey led his forces against the Hasmonean House. The Herodians were appointed as puppet rulers and maintained oversight from 63 BC to AD 135. The first was Antipater, who was succeeded by another Antipater, and he by his son Herod the Great, who ruled 37–4 BC.

Herod the Great was a wild, cunning man of insatiable ambition. During his period of prosperity, 25–13 BC, he rebuilt the temple; built cities, theaters, and other extravagant buildings; introduced Roman culture; and curried Roman friendship to the dismay of the Pharisees. His later years were spent with domestic discord and slander. His position became shaky, which perhaps explains his reaction to the report of the birth of Jesus. Herod died in 4 BC, and his kingdom was divided: Archelaus ruled Judea from 4 BC to AD 6. Herod Antipater governed Galilee from 4 BC to AD 39. Philip took control of Iturea from 4 BC to AD 34.

RELIGIOUS DEVELOPMENTS

By the time the New Testament canon was opened, Judaism subscribed to the centrality and authority of the Torah, observed the sacrificial services of the temple, and believed that God's kingdom would center in Palestine. But party differences had arisen over how these tenets of faith should be interpreted.

The Sadducees came from the priestly families. They claimed strict adherence to the Torah—so strict that they rejected the doctrine of the resurrection because they found no evidence for it in the Torah. Yet because they were interested in the priestly status quo, they advocated a degree of compromise with Hellenism, *if* the temple services were to continue.

On the other hand, the Pharisees, the largest and most influential group, abided by strict separatist practices: dietary rules, circumcision, fasting, and prayer. They wanted nothing to do with Gentiles. Yet they accepted teachings of books in addition to the Torah and added a body of oral tradition called the Talmud.

The Zealots were closely related to the Pharisees in doctrine. But they were political activists much like the Maccabean revolutionaries. The Essenes were a radical order that totally withdrew from society. Their zeal for the Torah and for the apocalyptic kingdom led them to become an ascetic, celibate community of strict discipline as they awaited the coming kingdom.

Wherever 10 men could be found to form a congregation, synagogues were created as centers of prayer, worship, and instruction. Feasts still had to be observed in the temple, but the synagogue assumed centrality for social and educational life.

To this world, united under Roman rule yet divided by competing philosophies, Jesus came. Within this Jewish party system, Jesus revealed the essence of God, though the Jewish leaders generally missed it. Amid this religious confusion, the New Testament era emerged.

Kings and Prophets of Israel and Judah

Adapted from *Standard Bible Atlas*, © Standard Publishing.

ALTAR AND TABERNACLE

In Old Testament times, group worship centered in 3 memorable institutions: the altar, the tabernacle, and the temple. The altar was the institution of the patriarchal dispensation. The tabernacle was added in the Jewish dispensation. Later the temple replaced it. A fourth institution, the synagogue, came into being near the end of Old Testament times after the Israelites had been taken into captivity.

——— THE ALTAR ———

A. THE IMPORTANCE OF THE ALTAR

The altar is important because it taught that restoring a relationship with God required blood sacrifice. While it may seem cruel to require the life of an animal as an act of worship, that does not compare to the real cost of rebellion against God. Animal sacrifice was only a reminder that God was willing to accept a substitute to take the death penalty for sin—treason against God. The fair penalty is death of the traitor—and that's all of us! Sacrifice was an ugly, bloody, messy affair.

It is quite possible that sacrifice began with Adam. It makes sense that God instituted sacrifice when making animal-skin clothing for Adam and Eve. Covering sin required sacrifice. The custom of the Hebrew patriarchs—Abraham, Isaac, and Jacob—was to build a rough stone altar wherever they camped. God commanded that the stone of the altars not be carved or decorated. Altars were not pretty! No human work or artistry could make a place of sacrifice more acceptable to God.

While the Israelites were in the wilderness after leaving Egypt, they made an altar of wood and brass or bronze that could be carried with them in their wanderings. This was placed in the courtyard of the tabernacle. When a permanent temple was built, there was a massive altar of natural (uncut and undecorated) stone in its courtyard.

B. USE OF THE ALTAR

Sacrifices of various kinds were burned in a wood fire on the altar. They may be divided into 2 classes:

1. *Sacrifices made to atone for sin and seek forgiveness.* Among these were the burnt offerings, sin offerings, and trespass offerings. Such sacrifices have been replaced by the sacrifice of Christ to atone for the sins of the world.

2. *Sacrifices made to express thanksgiving, devotion, and fellowship with God.* Among these were the peace offering and the grain offering. Forgiveness required blood sacrifice—the price of *life* itself. But the forgiven believer then dedicates his or her *livelihood* to the work

of God. With a similar purpose the Christian presents his or her body as a living sacrifice in unselfish living and service (Romans 12), offers praise to God (Hebrews 13:15), and gives sacrificially to those in need (v. 16).

—— THE TABERNACLE ——

When the people of Israel came out of Egypt, they were ready to begin their life as an independent nation. At Mount Sinai God gave them the law they were to live by. He also gave instructions for building a tabernacle to symbolize His dwelling among His people and to serve as a center of worship.

A. MATERIALS OF THE TABERNACLE

The Hebrew word for *tabernacle* is the common word for "tent." The tabernacle was God's tent in the midst of the tents of His people. Like the tents of the people, it could be easily taken down and moved. This was necessary because the nation was just starting on its long journey to the promised land.

The walls of the tabernacle were of fabric over a wooden frame. The roof was of fabric and skins. The fence around the large court was of fabric supported by wooden posts. Nevertheless, the structure was costly, symbolizing the willing devotion of God's people. Fabrics were richly embroidered; wooden parts were covered with gold, silver, or brass. The people had brought these precious materials out of Egypt with them (Exodus 11:2; 12:35, 36).

B. PLAN OF THE TABERNACLE

God gave Moses directions for building the tabernacle and warned him to follow those exactly (Exodus 25:9). One reason for such care, no doubt, was that the tabernacle was to be a symbol of the church that was to come centuries later (Hebrews 8:1, 2; 10:1). Details of the symbolism are not given in Scripture (9:5), but are generally taken to be as suggested below:

1. *The court,* or yard, around the tabernacle measured 150 by 75 feet. It is taken as a symbol of the world.

2. *The altar of burnt offering* (or sacrifice) was 7 ½ feet square and 4 ½ feet high. Sacrifices were burned on it, symbolizing the sacrifice of Christ for the sins of the world.

3. *The laver* was a large basin where the priests washed their hands and feet before going into the holy place. It is a symbol of Christian baptism.

4. *The holy place,* 30 by 15 feet, symbolized the church separated from the world (the court) and entered by way of Christ's sacrifice (the altar) and baptism (the laver).

5. *The table of showbread* (also called the bread of the Presence), on which 12 loaves were placed every week, was a symbol of the Lord's Supper.

6. *The candlestick,* more properly a lamp stand holding 7 lamps, gave light for the holy place. Thus it was a symbol of God's Word, which enlightens the church.

7. *The altar of incense* provided a place where incense was burned. The sweet-smelling smoke ascended like the prayers of God's people.

8. *The veil* was a curtain between the holy place and the most holy place (sometimes called the holy of holies). It symbolized the separation between Heaven and the Christians on earth.

9. *The most holy place*—a perfect cube at 15 feet long, wide, and high—was a symbol of Heaven, the particular place of God's presence.

10. *The ark of the covenant* was a wooden chest covered with gold and having a golden lid

bearing 2 golden cherubim. The ark contained 3 items: the 10 Commandments, symbolizing God's government; a dish of manna, recalling God's providence; and Aaron's rod, a reminder of God's power among His people (see Hebrews 9:4). Once a year the high priest sprinkled the top of the ark with blood, a symbol of Christ's blood by which we are cleansed.

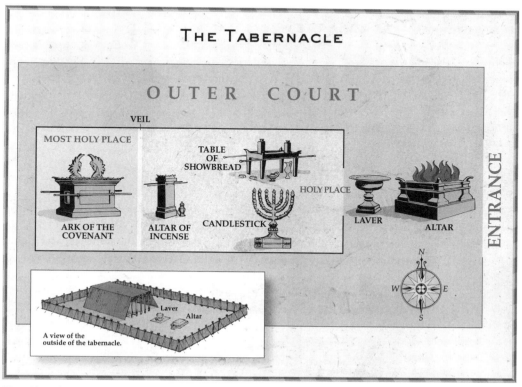

Adapted from *Old Testament Maps and Charts*, © Standard Publishing.

MAIN IDEAS OF THIS LESSON

The altar shows that restoring a relationship with God requires a _____

_____.

The tabernacle illustrated that God was _____ among His

_____.

QUESTIONS FOR DEEPER CONSIDERATION AND DISCUSSION

1. The Bible makes a distinction between sacrifice that pays the price for sin and a sacrifice to further the work of God on earth. How was that distinction made in the 2 types of offerings made in the Old Testament? How is Paul saying something similar in Ephesians 2:1-10?

2. Name 10 parts of the tabernacle and furnishings and tell what each may symbolize.

TEMPLE AND SYNAGOGUE

—— THE TEMPLE ——

For about 500 years, from the time of Moses to the time of Solomon, the tabernacle was Israel's place of worship. During this time the people left their tents and occupied well-built villages and cities in the promised land. After Jerusalem became the capital city, David thought of building a temple there to replace the tabernacle. After David's death, his son Solomon directed the building of the temple David had planned. This temple later was rebuilt and then extensively remodeled, but all of them were built on the same site and all had at their center a reproduction of the tabernacle with the holy place and the most holy place.

Adapted from *Standard Bible Atlas*, © Standard Publishing.

A. 3 TEMPLES

1. *Solomon's temple* was finished about 960 BC. Its ground plan was the same as that of the tabernacle; but the measurements were doubled, and the building was made of stone and cedar instead of fabrics. This temple stood nearly 400 years before Nebuchadnezzar's men destroyed it.

2. *Zerubbabel's temple* was built between 536 and 516 BC, after the Israelites returned from captivity in Babylon. Zerubbabel was the governor of Jerusalem who directed the work. His temple was at least as large as Solomon's, but not likely so richly adorned with gold. It lacked the ark of the covenant (which most scholars believe had been destroyed by the Babylonians). This temple was not destroyed as the first was, but after 500 years it was thoroughly rebuilt by Herod the Great, who ruled in Palestine when Jesus was born.

3. *Herod's temple* was the result of the rebuilding program begun by Herod about 20 BC. To avoid a general destruction of the old temple, the rebuilding was done a little at a time. It took only a year and a half to complete the temple itself, reproducing the form of the ancient tabernacle. But work on the surrounding buildings went on for years. The whole structure was not completed until about AD 64, only 6 years before the Romans finally destroyed it. During the ministry of Jesus, it was said that the temple had been 46 years in building (John 2:20). This temple was destroyed in AD 70 by Rome.

B. PLAN OF HEROD'S TEMPLE

Since Herod's temple was the temple we read about in the New Testament, we should know something about the plan of it, which of course, was similar to that of the earlier temples.

1. The holy place and the most holy place still preserved the shape of the original tabernacle, though they had the larger size of Solomon's temple. At the east end of the holy place, an elaborate porch rose high in the air. On the other 3 sides there were rooms, probably used by the priests for various purposes.

2. Around this central structure was the court of priests, enclosing the laver and the big altar at which the priests offered sacrifices.

3. Around the court of priests was the court of Israel, in which the men of Israel brought their sacrifices to the priests.

4. East of this court was the court of women, about 300 feet square, where both men and women of Israel gathered for their group worship. Around the outside of this court were rooms for meetings or for storage.

5. Outside this was the large court of Gentiles, nearly 900 feet square. This court was open to anyone, Jewish or foreign. This was where Jesus found the merchants selling sheep, cattle, and doves that might be offered in sacrifice. Along the walls were roofed areas, or porches, where people and animals could find shelter from rain or sun. At the northwest corner was a stronghold where soldiers were quartered, ready to put down any riot or rebellion that might arise when throngs gathered in the court.

───── THE SYNAGOGUE ─────

A. ORIGIN AND PURPOSE

Synagogue is literally a place where people are "led together." Unlike the altar, tabernacle, and temple, we see no biblical command to build synagogues. Like modern-day church buildings, synagogues were created for convenience, not because God directly commanded them to be built.

The synagogue probably began during the Babylonian captivity when the temple was in ruins. Unable to go to Jerusalem to worship, the Jews kept their ancient faith alive by meeting for worship and teaching in the various towns where they were forced to live. There was only 1 temple for the whole nation, but each community could have a synagogue. Synagogues are mentioned frequently in the New Testament, and Jesus worshipped in synagogues. During the missionary journeys of Paul, the synagogues were often the places in which the gospel was first preached.

B. USES OF THE SYNAGOGUE

The synagogue served important functions in the Jewish community. The synagogue was a *Bible school* where the Scriptures were taught and a *house of worship* for the Sabbath and other occasions. In addition, the synagogue was a *day school* in which children were taught the Scriptures along with reading and writing.

C. OFFICERS OF THE SYNAGOGUE

Each community had a council of elders known as *rulers* of the synagogue. They directed the services and also acted as town council and court. The *ministers* of the synagogue helped with the services, took care of the buildings, and sometimes were schoolteachers. The *batlanim* (bat-lah-neem, "men of leisure") were men who had some leisure time to give to the affairs of synagogue and community.

MAIN IDEAS OF THIS LESSON

While there were _____ different temples in biblical history, all of them were built on the same _____ and all had at their center a reproduction of the _____ with the holy place and the most holy place.

The synagogue probably began during the _____ captivity when the _____ was in ruins.

QUESTIONS FOR DEEPER CONSIDERATION AND DISCUSSION

1. Herod's temple consisted of 5 concentric areas. Name them. During the Babylonian captivity, the prophet Ezekiel saw a vision of a river coming from the temple, growing wider and deeper the farther it traveled (Ezekiel 47:1-12). How is that vision similar to the temple structure?

2. Although we have no biblical record of God commanding synagogues to be built, explain why you believe it was within God's will for them to be built. What are some practices of the church today that began for convenience, not because of a specific command? What should be our attitude toward such practices?

THE JEWISH FEASTS

As in all cultures, the Jews celebrated special days during the course of a year. In patriarchal times, the Israelites considered that the year ended when the last of the fruits were gathered in the fall, and the new year then began with the fall plowing and planting. The first month corresponded roughly to October. But when the Israelites left Egypt, God said the month of their *liberation* should be the first month. In the Bible the months are numbered on that basis, so the first month corresponds to April and the seventh month to October. However, the older calendar continued to be used in many civil and personal affairs, and the Jewish New Year still is celebrated in the fall.

But the Jewish feasts did more than mark the seasons. These celebrations were Old Testament institutions that help the Jews understand both past and future acts of God.

NAMES OF THE FEASTS

A. 2 TYPES OF FEASTS

There are 6 important Old Testament feasts—3 great feasts and 3 lesser feasts. The great feasts are also called the pilgrimage feasts. That is because Jews were expected to travel to the temple to celebrate Passover, Pentecost, and Tabernacles. The remaining 3 feasts—Trumpets, Dedication, and Purim—could be celebrated anywhere.

B. NATURE OF THE FEASTS

The nature of these feasts tells us much about the relationship of God and His people. First, they recognize times when God entered and altered history on behalf of those He loved. God is not distant and passive. He has broken into time and space to do great things!

Also the feasts are participatory. When God acts, He invites His people to join Him! Elements of the feast require participants to act out the historical event in some way, because God is just as present now as He was when the event first happened! And of course, the very nature of a feast shows that meeting with God is cause for celebration.

Finally, the pilgrimage feasts told of an even greater time yet to come. All 3 of the great feasts tell us something about the Messiah and His church.

THE PURPOSE OF THE FEASTS

A. PASSOVER (PESACH)

The Passover was celebrated at the end of the fourteenth day of the first month and the beginning of the fifteenth. (The new day began at sunset.) It began the weeklong Feast of Unleavened Bread, and the whole week came to be known as the Passover. The Passover originated when the Israelites were liberated from Egypt. Just before they left, God passed over the land to bring death to the firstborn of every Egyptian home, but He passed over the

Israelites without harm. Each family had a lamb for the ceremonial Passover dinner (also called a seder); or 2 or more small families might share a lamb. This feast came just before the barley harvest, and the first sheaf of the harvest was given as an offering. After the temple was built, the nation gathered there for the feast. To this day those celebrating a seder transport themselves back to the first Passover with the words, "Why is this night different from all other nights?"

The Messianic implications of Passover are great. The New Testament recognizes Jesus as the Passover lamb whose death finally causes death to pass over humankind once and for all. Jesus was crucified during the celebration of this feast!

B. Pentecost (Feast of Weeks, Firstfruits, Wheat Harvest, Shavuot)

The Greek word *pentekoste* means "fiftieth day." Pentecost was the fiftieth day after the Passover Sabbath. It is also called the Feast of Weeks because it came 7 weeks after the Passover. According to Jewish tradition, Pentecost is the anniversary of the giving of the law at Sinai. After the temple was built, the people of Israel gathered there for Pentecost. Barley and wheat were harvested between Passover and Pentecost, so thanksgiving was a feature of the second feast. This was symbolized by an offering of loaves of bread. To this day the 10 Commandments are read in synagogues as celebrants receive the law just as their ancestors did.

It is no accident that the church began on Pentecost. Moses brought the law down from Sinai so God's people may *know* His will. The Holy Spirit descended on Pentecost to empower Christians to *do* His will.

C. Tabernacles (Booths, Ingathering, Sukkot)

The Feast of Tabernacles began on the fifteenth of the seventh month (about October) and lasted a week. This feast was also called the Feast of Ingathering because it came after all the fruits of the year had been gathered in. In a way it corresponded to our Thanksgiving. More significantly, however, this feast commemorated the years of wandering in the wilderness. To remind them of those wilderness days, the people left their houses and lived in temporary shelters made of branches. These were called tabernacles, or booths, and that name was given to the feast.

Other elements of this feast include remembering the pillar of fire that the Jews followed in the wilderness and the water gushing out of the rock at Moses' command. Typically, participants waved palm branches and recited Psalm 118:26—"Blessed be he that cometh in the name of the Lord." This was also a time for celebrants to welcome and expect special guests.

The climax of the Gospel of John occurs at a celebration of Tabernacles (John 7, 8). Jesus identified himself as the light of the world (referring to the pillar of fire) and the giver of living water. We also see elements of this feast take place when Jesus entered Jerusalem on what we now call Palm Sunday, even though it was not the season for this feast. The palm branches, shouting the words of Psalm 118:26, and welcoming a holy visitor to Jerusalem are elements of Tabernacles and identify Jesus as the Messiah.

D. The 3 lesser feasts

The Feast of Trumpets came on the first day of the seventh month. It was New Year's Day by the ancient patriarchal calendar. Modern Jews call it Rosh Hashanah, or Jewish New Year.

The Feast of Dedication is also known as the Festival of Lights and Hanukkah. It was a weeklong festival beginning on the twenty-fifth of the ninth month. This festival had its beginning in the time between the Old Testament and the New, when the temple was purified and rededicated after invading Syrians had defiled it.

Purim fell on the fourteenth and fifteenth of the twelfth month. It commemorated Queen Esther's deliverance of her people from the massacre planned by Haman. The name *Purim* means "lots," recalling that Haman cast lots to decide when he would destroy the Jews (Esther 3:7).

E. THE DAY OF ATONEMENT (YOM KIPPUR)

The Day of Atonement was the tenth day of the seventh month. It was not a feast day but a day of fasting and penitence. Special offerings were made to atone for sins.

Understanding the Old Testament feasts also helps us understand the New Testament ordinances of baptism and the Lord's Supper. Note that both of these, like Old Testament feast days, recall how God acted in history and require participants to act out the event. In baptism, a candidate physically identifies with the death, burial, and resurrection of Jesus by being "buried" in water and being "resurrected" from it. In the Lord's Supper we testify that we want to internalize Jesus by eating the elements and thereby recognize that all who do so are part of the body of Christ, the church.

MAIN IDEAS OF THIS LESSON

The 3 great feasts, or pilgrimage feasts, of the Jews are

_____, _____,

and_____ .

The 3 minor feasts are _____,

_____ , and_____ .

QUESTIONS FOR DEEPER CONSIDERATION AND DISCUSSION

1. Consider the 3 great feasts. Tell how each relates to Christ and His church.

2. Why do you think God has His people act out His important deeds rather than just talk about them? How does understanding this aspect of Jewish feasts help make baptism and the Lord's Supper more meaningful to you?

WRITTEN FOR OUR ADMONITION

Sometimes Christians question the value of studying the Old Testament. "We belong to the new covenant," they say. "Why study all this stuff about law and sacrifices and the like? We want to know about Jesus and grace!" But the New Testament frequently cites the Old Testament. Paul said, "These things happened unto them for ensamples: and they are written for our admonition" (1 Corinthians 10:11). If we would know of Jesus and grace, the Old Testament is a good place to start!

Old Testament Event	New Testament References
God calls Moses	Acts 7:30-34. Stephen cites the call of Moses in his defense before the council.
The Passover	1 Corinthians 5:7. Jesus is "our passover" (see also 1 Peter 1:19).
Crossing the Red Sea	1 Corinthians 10:1, 2. Israel "passed through the sea."
The Law given through Moses	Mark 7:9, 10. Jesus quotes one of the 10 Commandments as a "commandment of God" and as the words of Moses (see also John 1:17; 7:19).
Israel to be a "kingdom of priests, and a holy nation"	1 Peter 2:9 paraphrases Exodus 19:6 in reference to Christians.
Building the tabernacle	Hebrews 9 describes the tabernacle as having "patterns" of heavenly things (v. 23).
Israel led by pillar of cloud/fire	1 Corinthians 10:1, 2. Israel was "under the cloud."
Rebellion in the desert	1 Corinthians 10:5-13 describes Israel's repeated rebellion (see also John 3:14; Acts 7:39-43; Hebrews 3:15–4:6).
The greatest commandment	Mark 12:28-34. Jesus cites Deuteronomy 6:4, 5 as the "first" of all the commandments (see also Matthew 4:10; Luke 10:25-27).
The fall of Jericho	Hebrews 11:30, 31 says it was faith that brought down the walls of Jericho, noting also the faith of Rahab in hiding the spies (see also James 2:25).

Adapted from *Standard Bible Atlas,* © Standard Publishing.

NEW TESTAMENT LANDS

Most of Jesus' earthly life was spent in Palestine, a little area east of the Mediterranean Sea. Acts and the New Testament letters bring us to other lands east and north of the Mediterranean.

—— PALESTINE ——

A. BOUNDARIES AND TERRITORIES

The Mediterranean coast made up a great part of the western boundary of Palestine, and *the Jordan River* formed the boundary to the east. *The Sea of Galilee* lay at the northern end of the Jordan, and the Dead Sea lay at its southern end.

Three territories lay on the eastern side of the Jordan and are given some mention in the New Testament. *Perea* occupied the eastern side of the Jordan River valley, from about a third of the way down from the Sea of Galilee to about a third of the way down the eastern shore of the Dead Sea. It did not extend too far inland. Israelites of the tribes Reuben, Gad, and Manasseh occupied this area in Old Testament times.

The *Decapolis* was a group of 10 cities lying to the north and east of Perea. The 10 cities were not an official political unit, but they were grouped together because of their language, culture, and location. They were founded during the Greek Empire and had a strong Greek culture. North of the Decapolis lay the tetrarchy of Philip, lands that make up parts of modern-day Syria and Lebanon.

The 3 territories west of the Jordan are much more prominently featured in the New Testament. *Judea* lay in the south, with its northern border about a third of the way up from the Dead Sea to the Sea of Galilee. *Galilee* was the large northern area surrounding the sea named for it. Galilee was mostly rocky country and was a major location for much of Jesus' ministry. Between Judea and Galilee lay *Samaria*. Samaritans were Jews who intermarried with their Assyrian captives after the northern kingdom of Israel fell in the 8th century BC. Such hostility existed between Jews and Samaritans during Jesus' day that most Jews traveling between Judea and Galilee would cross over to the eastern side of the Jordan River to avoid traveling through Samaria.

B. IMPORTANT CITIES

Jerusalem, Bethlehem, Bethany, and *Jericho* were cities in Judea. Jerusalem remained the capital of Judea. Bethany was a small village outside Jerusalem and was home to Jesus' friends Mary, Martha, and Lazarus. Bethlehem was the hometown of King David and birthplace of Jesus. It was 6 miles south of Jerusalem. Jesus visited Jericho late in His ministry, and the dangers of the road connecting Jericho and Jerusalem provided the setting of Jesus' famous parable of the Good Samaritan.

Nazareth, Cana, and *Capernaum* were in Galilee. Jesus grew up in Nazareth, performed His first miracle in Cana, and centered His ministry in Capernaum on the northwest shore of the Sea of Galilee.

Bethsaida, Caesarea Philippi, and *Gergesa* were in the tetrarchy of Philip. It was in a wilderness near Bethsaida that Jesus fed the 5,000.

—— THE MEDITERRANEAN WORLD ——

The church was born on the Day of Pentecost in the city of Jerusalem. In less than 3 decades, churches were founded all over the Mediterranean world.

A. THE FIRST YEARS OF THE CHURCH

Jesus commanded the disciples to be His witnesses "in Jerusalem, and in all Judaea, and in Samaria, and unto the uttermost part of the earth" (Acts 1:8). Yet for the first few years, the church remained in Jerusalem. Persecution forced the church from her comfort zone, and soon the gospel spread through Judea, into Samaria, and north into the land of the Greeks. It was in the Syrian town of Antioch that the believers were first called Christians. After Saul of Tarsus became a Christian, he (then known as Paul) ministered in the church in Antioch.

B. THE JOURNEYS OF PAUL

Paul made 3 notable missionary journeys starting from Antioch, and he later made a voyage from Caesarea to Rome. His first journey took him only as far as the southwestern areas of modern-day Turkey. The following 2 journeys took him into modern-day Greece. Finally, after his arrest, Paul was taken to stand trial in Rome. The book of Acts begins in Jerusalem and ends in the most powerful city of the ancient world.

MAIN IDEAS OF THIS LESSON

Most of Jesus' ministry took place in the 3 provinces of Palestine west of the Jordan River:
_____, _____, and
_____.

The church began in _____. Largely because of the
_____ missionary journeys of the apostle _____, the gospel was spread in the major cities in the Mediterranean world, including Rome.

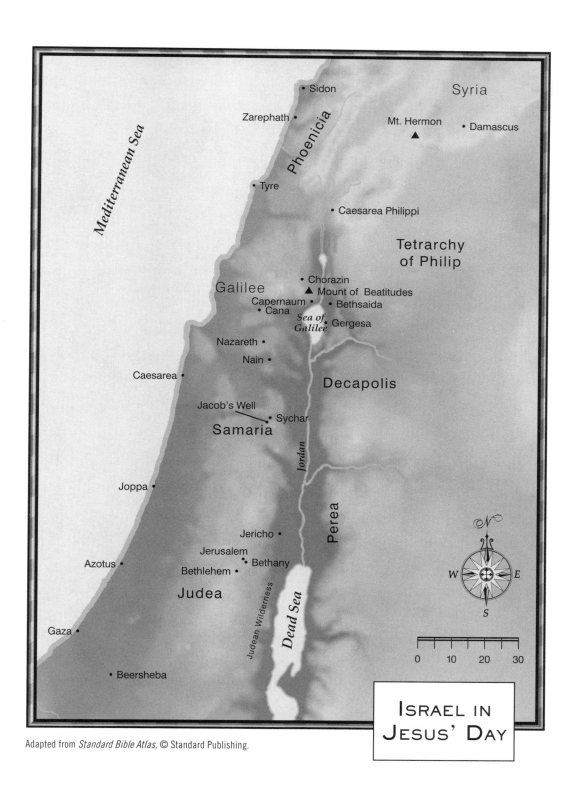

Mediterranean Sea

Sidon

Syria

Zarephath

Phoenicia

Mt. Hermon ▲

Damascus

Tyre

Caesarea Philippi

Tetrarchy
of Philip

Galilee

Chorazin
▲ Mount of Beatitudes
Capernaum
Cana
Bethsaida
Sea of
Galilee
Gergesa

Nazareth

Nain

Caesarea

Decapolis

Jacob's Well

Sychar

Samaria

Jordan

Joppa

Perea

Jericho

Jerusalem
Bethany

Azotus

Bethlehem

Judea

Judean Wilderness

Dead Sea

Gaza

N

W
E

S

0   10   20   30

Beersheba

ISRAEL IN
JESUS' DAY

Adapted from *Standard Bible Atlas,* © Standard Publishing.

NEW TESTAMENT WORLD

Black Sea

PONTUS

BITHYNIA

CAPPADOCIA

SYRIA

Antioch
Seleucia
Damascus
Tarsus
CILICIA
Tyre
Sidon
Jordan
Dead Sea
Caesarea
Jerusalem
JUDEA

GALATIA
Antioch
PISIDIA
Iconium
Derbe
Lystra
PHRYGIA
PAMPHILIA
Perga
Attalia
Patara
Myra

ASIA
Ephesus
Miletus

CYPRUS
Salamis
Paphos

RHODES
CNIDUS

Mediterranean Sea

EGYPT
Nile
Alexandria

THRACE

MACEDONIA
Philippi
Neapolis
Troas
Thessalonica
Berea

Aegean
Sea

Athens
ACHAIA
Corinth
Cenchrea

CRETE
Lasea
Fair Havens

Cyrene
CYRENE

ILLYRICUM

Adriatic Sea

Rhegium

ITALY
Rome
Puteoli
Three
Taverns
Forum of
Appius

SICILY
Syracuse

MALTA
(MELITA)

0 80 160 240

W N E S

Adapted from *Standard Bible Atlas,* © Standard Publishing.

THE CHRIST IN PROPHECY

—— PROPHECIES OF THE CHRIST ——

A. NUMBER AND KINDS OF PROPHECIES

Scholars have identified hundreds of prophecies in the Old Testament concerning Jesus. Three kinds of prophecies should be mentioned:

1. *Types*—A type (or typology) is a person, event, or practice in the Old Testament that gives an example of what the Messiah would do. For example, Joseph is seen as a type of Christ because he was thrown into a pit by his own people but returned as a ruler. Noah's ark and the flood can be seen as foreshadowing Jesus's saving from judgment those who remain in Him. The Passover celebration is a typology of the final Passover lamb, Jesus himself.

2. *Obscure prophecies*—Directed by the Holy Spirit, New Testament writers revealed how statements referring to an event of the past should be seen as the prophecy of another. Hosea spoke of God leading Israel out of Egypt (Hosea 11:1), but Matthew tells us that this prophecy was also fulfilled when Mary and Joseph fled with Jesus to Egypt shortly after His birth (Matthew 2:15).

3. *Plain statements*—Some prophets spoke clearly about a coming king. Isaiah prophesied about someone he identified as the "servant" (Isaiah 42:1). Jeremiah foretold a coming "Branch of righteousness" (Jeremiah 33:15) and a future "new covenant" (31:31). Daniel predicted a king that he described as "the stone [that] was cut out of the mountain without hands" (Daniel 2:45).

B. WRITERS AND TIME OF THE PROPHECIES

The prophecies about Christ were not all written by 1 man, but were given through Moses, David, Isaiah, Jeremiah, Daniel, Micah, Malachi, and others. These prophecies were not all written at the same time. Those of Moses were written nearly 1,500 years before Christ came, those of David about 1,000 years before Christ came, those of Isaiah more than 700 years before Christ came, and those of Malachi about 400 years before Christ came. These prophecies are not in just a single book or section of the Old Testament but run throughout. The first prophecy in the Old Testament is that of the seed of the woman in Genesis 3:15; the last is that of the Sun of righteousness in Malachi 4:2.

C. DIFFICULTY OF UNDERSTANDING

Prophecies about the Christ were understood so poorly that the leading scholars of His people did not recognize Him when He came. Of course, typologies and obscure prophecies would have been difficult to understand until seen in the light of their fulfillment. That is understandable. Furthermore, sometimes no distinction was made between Christ's first coming in humility and His later return in glory, contributing to confusion.

But often, selfishness and stubbornness played a role in this lack of understanding. Many Jewish students loved the prophecies of glory but ignored or misunderstood the prophecies of humility and suffering. People seeking healing, such as the blind men on the road to Jericho, knew that Jesus was the promised Son of David (Matthew 20:29-34) and fully expected Him to heal as Isaiah had predicted centuries earlier (Isaiah 29:17-19). But the leaders, fearful of having their power threatened, were willing to kill Jesus, even though His miracles clearly revealed His identity (John 11:45-53).

SPECIFIC EXAMPLES OF PROPHECY

Studying several key examples may help us understand more about Old Testament prophecies concerning the Christ. Look up these passages:

Hope in the garden (Genesis 3:15)—Even when pronouncing judgment on humankind due to the rebellion of Adam and Eve, God told of coming hope. The serpent would bite the offspring of the woman, but the offspring would crush the serpent underfoot. In strictly physical terms, this played out over and over again in human history—a snake would strike and be killed. But since the serpent was the tempter in the Garden of Eden, this was a promise of Christ, who would destroy the works of the devil and the devil himself.

The ultimate king (Genesis 49:10)—Nearly 2,000 years before Christ, Jacob predicted that the royal line of Israel would be that of his son Judah. Furthermore, he predicted the coming of "Shiloh" (from the Hebrew word for "peace"), the true king of Israel and Prince of Peace.

A priest like Melchizedek (Genesis 14:18-20; Psalm 110:4)—After a great battle, Abraham gave a tenth of the spoils of war to a mysterious priest and king. King David prophesied that this priest and king was a typology of the coming Messiah.

A prophet like Moses (Deuteronomy 18:18)—While Moses ranks with the greatest figures in Old Testament history, he himself prophesied that a prophet would come who would be everything he was and more.

The peacemaker from Bethlehem (Micah 5:2-8)—During a time of political uncertainty, the prophet not only told of a coming Prince of Peace but also named His birthplace 7 centuries before Christ.

The Son of God (Psalm 2)—This great prophetic song sings of the coming anointed one (Messiah) and identifies Him as the Son of God.

God with us (Isaiah 7:14)—When King Ahaz of Judah was looking for political solutions to bring peace, the prophet told him that God was with His people now and would ultimately send Immanuel, the Messiah, who would carry God's very presence to earth. Isaiah further identified Him as the "Wonderful, Counselor, The mighty God, The everlasting Father, The Prince of Peace" (9:6).

The healing servant (Isaiah 35:5, 6)—The rebellion of Adam and Eve brought death and suffering. Isaiah promised a coming servant who would heal what had been broken.

The suffering servant (Isaiah 53)—This healing and peace would come at a tremendous cost. The servant would take the punishment we deserve and be an atoning offering for our sin.

The Son of man (Daniel 7:13, 14)—Daniel told of someone who would have authority, not just over Israel but also over all nations. He had the appearance of an ordinary man but would rule forever in an eternal kingdom.

—— CONCLUSION ——

It is not to be believed that men by human power alone could look hundreds of years into the future and foretell such details accurately. But God guided the prophets, and God knows the future as well as the past.

MAIN IDEAS OF THIS LESSON

Three kinds of Messianic prophecies are _____ (events, people, and practices that foreshadowed the work of Jesus), _____ prophecies that were only understood after Christ's coming, and _____ statements that clearly predicted a coming Savior.

The first prophecy of Jesus (Genesis 3:15) is the prediction of the _____ of the woman. The final Old Testament prophecy (Malachi 4:2) tells of the coming Sun of _____ .

QUESTIONS FOR DEEPER CONSIDERATION AND DISCUSSION

1. There are hundreds of Old Testament prophecies about Jesus. But the very nation to whom those prophecies were given did not recognize Jesus as the Messiah at first. What are some reasons for this?

2. Review the specific prophecies about Jesus listed in this lesson. Which is the most remarkable to you? Explain why you find it so convincing.

OTHER MESSIANIC PROPHECIES

Event	Where Predicted	How Fulfilled
Jesus would minister in Galilee.	Isaiah 9:1, 2	Matthew 4:12-16
Jesus would enter Jerusalem in triumph.	Zechariah 9:9	Matthew 21:4, 5
A friend would betray Jesus.	Psalm 41:9	John 13:18
The price would be 30 silver pieces.	Zechariah 11:12, 13	Matthew 27:3-10
Jesus would endure mockery.	Psalm 22:7, 8	Matthew 27:41-43
Evil men would gamble for Jesus' garments.	Psalm 22:18	John 19:23, 24
Jesus' hands and feet were to be pierced.	Psalm 22:16	John 20:20, 25, 27
No bone of Jesus' body would be broken.	Psalm 34:20	John 19:36
Tormentors would pierce Jesus' body.	Zechariah 12:10	John 19:37
Jesus would be buried with the rich.	Isaiah 53:9	Matthew 27:57-60

LIFE OF CHRIST—PART 1

—— AN OVERVIEW OF ——
NEW TESTAMENT HISTORY

New Testament history can be divided into 3 periods:

1. *The earthly life of Christ* was from about 6–4 BC to AD 30. The date of His birth is about 6–4 BC by our calendar because a mistake was made when this calendar was first started. The makers of the calendar thought Jesus was born later than He really was. This period is recorded in the four Gospels.

2. *The beginnings of the church* include the years from AD 30 to 45, during which the gospel spread from Jerusalem through Judea and Samaria, reached to the Gentile Cornelius at Caesarea, and won many Gentiles to Christ in Antioch. This history is recorded in Acts 1–12.

3. *The expansion of the apostolic church* reaches from about AD 45 to 100. Paul began his first missionary journey about AD 47. Other disciples were scattered in various places throughout the world. The last living apostle, John, finished his writing and his life about AD 100. Some of these stories are found in Acts 13–28 and in the writings of Paul, Peter, Jude, and John.

The earthly life of Christ may be divided into 7 periods:

- 30 years of youth (period of preparation)
- first year of ministry (period of obscurity)
- second year of ministry (period of popularity)
- third year of ministry (period of opposition)
- last 3 months (period of persecution)
- last week (Passion Week)
- 40 days (resurrection appearances)

The first 2 of these periods will be covered in this lesson, and the remaining 5 will be covered in lessons 19 and 20.

—— 30 YEARS OF YOUTH ——
(PERIOD OF PREPARATION)

Memorize these 5 events of the first 30 years of Jesus' life:

1. *Birth* (Luke 2:1-20)—Jesus was born in Bethlehem, a small town about 6 miles south of Jerusalem, though the home of Joseph and Mary was in Nazareth, several days' journey away. Prophecy was fulfilled when Jesus was born in Bethlehem (Micah 5:2), born of a virgin (Isaiah 7:14), and was descended from Abraham, Judah, and David.

2. *Flight* (Matthew 2:1-15)—When King Herod heard that a new king had been born in Bethlehem, he determined to kill the child. Instructed by an angel, Joseph took the baby Jesus

and His mother and fled to Egypt. Herod's slaughter of the other babies of Bethlehem fulfilled prophecy (see Jeremiah 31:15; Matthew 2:16-18).

3. *Return* (Matthew 2:19-23)—When Herod died, Joseph and Mary brought Jesus back from Egypt and returned to their home in Nazareth, again fulfilling prophecy (Hosea 11:1; Matthew 2:15). Of Jesus' youth we know only 1 other event—His trip to Jerusalem at the age of 12, where He amazed the scholars with His knowledge. After that He "increased in wisdom and stature, and in favor with God and man" (see Luke 2:40-52).

4. *Baptism* (Matthew 3:13-17)—John the Baptist, forerunner of Jesus, was preaching repentance and baptizing people for repentance, in preparation for the coming Christ. He was baptizing in the Jordan River east of Jerusalem. Jesus came to be baptized, not because He had any sins to repent of, but in order to fulfill "all righteousness." Immediately after His baptism, "the heavens were opened unto him, and he saw the Spirit of God descending like a dove, and lighting upon him: and lo a voice from heaven, saying, This is my beloved Son, in whom I am well pleased." This was the first public announcement that Jesus was God's Son.

5. *Temptation* (Matthew 4:1-11)—Following His baptism, Jesus was led into the wilderness to be tempted of the devil, but He resisted every temptation. Jesus has been "in all points tempted like as we are, yet without sin" (Hebrews 4:15).

——— FIRST YEAR OF MINISTRY ——— (PERIOD OF OBSCURITY)

John is the only book that tells us much about this period of obscurity. Memorize these 5 events from the first year of Jesus' ministry:

1. *First miracle*—In Cana of Galilee, not far from His home and probably in the home of a kinsman or friend, Jesus turned water into wine (John 2:1-11).

2. *First cleansing of the temple*—John 2:13-16 tells how Jesus cleansed the temple for the first time. He cleansed it again a few days before His death. By driving out the merchants and money changers, He made the temple what it was designed to be—a place of prayer.

3. *Nicodemus*—This scholar and ruler came to Jesus by night and heard the first recorded discourse of our Lord. In it is the well-loved John 3:16. Read the rest in verses 1-21.

4. *Woman of Samaria*—Weary from travel and waiting for His dinner, Jesus forgot His own needs to give His attention to a woman of a despised race and bad reputation. Here is an example of personal evangelism (John 4:1-42).

5. *Nobleman's son*—Jesus healed this son without even going near him, giving us a remarkable demonstration of Jesus' power and the nobleman's faith (John 4:46-54).

MAIN IDEAS OF THIS LESSON

New Testament history can be divided into 3 periods: the earthly _____ of _____, the _____ of the _____, and the _____ of the apostolic _____.

The 5 main events in the first 30 years of Jesus' life (preparation) are _____, _____, _____, _____, and _____.

The 5 main events in the first year of Jesus' ministry (obscurity) are first _____, first _____ of the temple, _____, woman of _____, and _____ son.

JOHN—A WORKING OUTLINE

John outlined his Gospel around 7 miraculous signs that demonstrated that Jesus was who He claimed to be . . . and that cause us to B.E.L.I.E.V.E.

Born again (turning water into wine)

John the Baptist and his disciples (John 1:19-51; 3:22-36)
The signature miracle (John 2:1-11)
First clearing of the temple (John 2:12-25)
Dialogue with Nicodemus (John 3:1-21)
Samaritan woman (John 4:1-42)

Every nation (healing of the official's son)

Breaking barriers of time and space (John 4:43-54)
Parallel miracles (Matthew 8:5-13; Mark 7:24-30)

Lord of the Sabbath (healing at Bethesda pool)

Healing of disabled man (John 5:1-15)
Persecution because of Sabbath law (John 5:16-47)
Parallel discourses (Matthew 12:1-14; Luke 6:1-11)

Inexhaustible supply (feeding of 5,000)

Most famous miracle (John 6:1-15)
Bread of life dialogue (John 6:25-71)
Tabernacles dialogue and living water (John 7, 8)

Escape plan (walking on water)

Same miracle, different focus (John 6:16-24 vs. Matthew 14:22-36)
Tabernacles dialogue and light of the world (John 7, 8)

Visionary leadership (blind man and the pool of Siloam)

Miracle and its consequences (John 9)
Good Shepherd (John 10:1-21)
Festival of lights and Jewish leaders in darkness (John 10:22-42)

Eternal life (raising of Lazarus)

Unassailable miracle and its consequences (John 11—19)
Resurrection (John 20)
Forgiveness and restoration (John 21)

LIFE OF CHRIST—PART 2

Review the first 2 periods of Jesus' life, recalling 5 events in each. If necessary, refresh your memory by looking at lesson 18.

——— SECOND YEAR OF MINISTRY ——— (PERIOD OF POPULARITY)

Very many events of this year are recorded. Memorize these 5 events from the second year of Jesus' ministry:

1. *The calling of the fishermen*—Simon Peter, Andrew, James, and John were busy commercial fishermen whom Jesus called to follow Him (Matthew 4:18-22). At that time multitudes of people were thronging around Jesus to see His miracles and hear His teaching. Besides the 4 fishermen, He chose 8 more to form the circle of 12 apostles.

2. *The Sermon on the Mount*—To His chosen 12 and a great multitude, Jesus set forth the basic principles of life in His kingdom. In this sermon we find the well-known Beatitudes and the Lord's Prayer (Matthew 5–7). The theme of the sermon is that the righteousness that comes through Jesus by grace is greater than the righteousness gained by the type of law keeping the Jewish leaders advocated.

3. *The widow's son*—As Jesus was going throughout Galilee to teach and heal, He met a funeral procession coming out of the town of Nain. The dead man was a widow's son, and probably her only source of support. Jesus restored him to life (Luke 7:11-17).

4. *The lakeside parables*—Matthew 13 records 8 parables that Jesus seems to have told in a single day. These are also known as the kingdom parables because they tell about the coming kingdom of God, the church. At least some of them were told by the Sea of Galilee near Capernaum while Jesus sat in a boat and spoke to the people on the beach. Read these and practice telling them in your own words. They are:

- the parable of the sower
- the tares (weeds)
- the mustard seed
- the leaven (yeast)
- the treasure in the field
- the pearl of great price
- the net
- the householder

5. *Jairus's daughter*—In Capernaum Jesus raised Jairus's daughter from the dead (Matthew 9:18-26; Mark 5:21-43). Jairus was a man of prominence, and the fame of this miracle spread everywhere, although Jesus asked that no one be told.

THIRD YEAR OF MINISTRY
(PERIOD OF OPPOSITION)

The common people heard Jesus gladly, but many scholars and rulers opposed Him. Their opposition was due partly to jealousy and partly to their anger at His rebukes of their sins and hypocrisy. Memorize 5 of the recorded events of this period:

1. *Feeding the 5,000*—All 4 Gospels record this miracle. Jesus borrowed 5 loaves and 2 fish from a boy and used them to feed 5,000 men, plus women and children (Matthew 14:13-21).

2. *The Syrophoenician's daughter*—Withdrawing from the crowds of Galilee to have more time with His apostles, Jesus went northwest to the vicinity of Tyre and Sidon. There He healed the daughter of a foreign woman, though His mission at that time was mainly to the people of Israel (Mark 7:24-30).

3. *Peter's confession*—Many people supposed Jesus was a prophet, but His chosen 12 were convinced that He was the Christ, the Son of God. Peter voiced this belief in an impressive way (Matthew 16:13-17). But soon Peter would show that his understanding was still incomplete!

4. *The transfiguration*—A week after Peter's confession, Jesus took 3 disciples and sought solitude for a time on a high mountain. There He was transfigured, His face and His garments becoming a gleaming white. Before the eyes of the 3 disciples, Moses and Elijah appeared and talked with Jesus. Peter suggested building 3 shelters for Jesus, Moses, and Elijah; but the voice of God spoke to them, identifying Jesus as His Son to whom they should listen (Matthew 17:1-8).

5. *The Good Samaritan*—The well-known Good Samaritan in the parable is among the finest examples of neighborliness. Nevertheless, this story must have intensified the leaders' opposition to Jesus, for it pictured a despised Samaritan in more favorable light than 2 of their religious leaders (Luke 10:29-37).

MAIN IDEAS OF THIS LESSON

The 5 main events in the second year of Jesus' ministry (popularity) are the calling of the _____, the _____ on the Mount, the _____son, the _____ _____, and Jairus's _____.

The 5 main events in the third year of Jesus' ministry (opposition) are feeding the _____, _____ daughter, Peter's _____, the _____, and the Good _____ parable.

QUESTIONS FOR DEEPER CONSIDERATION AND DISCUSSION

1. After the healing of Jairus's daughter (as well as after some other healings during the year of popularity), Jesus commanded that those involved not tell anyone. Contrast this command to the

attitudes of human beings who are in the middle of a period of rising popularity. Why might Jesus have issued this strange command?

2. Who were the 2 Old Testament characters with Jesus on the mount of transfiguration? What might be the significance of those 2?

The City of Jerusalem

EVENTS CONCLUDING JESUS' MINISTRY

LIFE OF CHRIST—PART 3

Review the first 4 periods of Jesus' life, recalling 5 events in each. If necessary, refresh your memory by looking at lessons 18 and 19. We now continue with the last 3 periods.

—— LAST 3 MONTHS ——
(PERIOD OF PERSECUTION)

Some of the rulers had thought of killing Jesus before this, but now they were plotting against His life more actively and vigorously. Memorize 5 events of these 3 months:

1. *Raising of Lazarus*—About 2 miles from Jerusalem in Bethany, just over the Mount of Olives, was the home of Mary, Martha, and Lazarus. Jesus seemed at home there. Lazarus died, but after Lazarus had been in the tomb 4 days, Jesus raised him from death (John 11).

2. *10 healed of leprosy*—Leprosy was seldom cured. On this occasion Jesus healed 10 men of the disease, but only 1 was grateful enough to return and thank Him. The thankful man was not a Jew, but a member of the despised Samaritan people (Luke 17:11-19).

3. *Little children*—Knowing that Jesus was overworked, His disciples would have sent away the children who had come to see Him. But Jesus said, "Forbid them not, to come unto me; for of such is the kingdom of heaven" (Matthew 19:13-15). No doubt this Scripture is partly responsible for the care we give to children in our Sunday schools.

4. *Rich young ruler*—A rich young ruler with an exemplary reputation came to Jesus to ask about eternal life. Jesus made it very clear that anyone who would have eternal life must follow Him at all costs (Luke 18:18-27).

5. *Zaccheus*—A rich tax collector, too short to see over the heads of other people, climbed into a sycamore tree to see Jesus pass. His earnest zeal was rewarded when Jesus went to his home and the tax collector resolved to be honest and generous (Luke 19:1-10).

—— LAST WEEK (PASSION WEEK) ——

Memorize 5 events of the week that ended with Jesus' death:

1. *Mary's anointing*—Jesus was a supper guest in Bethany when Mary anointed Him with costly ointment (Matthew 26:6-13; Mark 14:3-9; John 12:1-8). This was probably on Friday or Saturday a week before His death. This act of faith showed that Mary understood something most of His followers did not—that Jesus had to die to pay for the sins of humankind.

2. *Triumphal entry*—On the first day of the week, Jesus entered Jerusalem as a king might enter in triumph, riding a young donkey while the people waved palm branches and sang praises (Matthew 21:1-11; Mark 11:1-11; Luke 19:28-44; John 12:12-16).

3. *10 virgins*—As He taught in the temple on Tuesday, Jesus told a parable in which He compared 10 bridesmaids awaiting the arrival of the bridegroom to believers awaiting His second coming. This parable, along with others told at the same time, warned the people to be ready for His return (Matthew 25:1-13).

4. *The upper room*—In an upper room in Jerusalem, Jesus ate the last supper with His disciples. There He instituted the Lord's Supper. This was Thursday night (Matthew 26:17-29).

5. *Crucifixion*—On false accusations and perjured testimony, Jesus was condemned to death, tortured, and nailed to a cross. In the midst of cruel taunts and terrible suffering, He prayed for His murderers and remembered to provide a home for His mother. Then He died for the sins of the world (Mark 14:53–15:39).

——— 40 DAYS (RESURRECTION ——— APPEARANCES)

During the 40 days between His resurrection and His ascension, Jesus appeared to disciples at least 10 times. Memorize these 5 appearances:

1. *Appearance to 2*—Jesus joined 2 disciples as they walked to Emmaus (Luke 24:13-32).

2. *Appearance to 10*—"The 11" was the name of the group as a group. But they were minus Thomas when Jesus appeared in their midst on this occasion (Luke 24:33-49). (In John 20:26-29, He appeared to the group when Thomas was present.)

3. *Appearance to 7*—By the Sea of Galilee, Jesus had breakfast with 7 apostles (John 21:1-14).

4. *Appearance to 500*—First Corinthians 15:6 tells us that Jesus was seen by more than 500 believers at once. Paul further stated that most of these were still alive at the time he wrote the letter, encouraging his readers to talk to them to check out the story!

5. *Appearance to 11*—Jesus met the 11 apostles in Galilee and commissioned them to take His gospel to the whole world (Matthew 28:16-20). Possibly it was at the same time that He was seen by 500. He appeared again to the 11 at the time of His ascension (Acts 1:10-13; Luke 24:50, 51).

MAIN IDEAS OF THIS LESSON

The 5 main events in the final 3 months of Jesus' ministry (persecution) are the raising of _____, _____ healed of leprosy, little _____, _____ young _____, and _____.

The 5 main events in the final week of Jesus' ministry (Passion Week) are Mary's _____, _____ entry, 10 _____, the upper _____, and _____.

Five key resurrection appearances of Jesus can be remembered by the number of people He appeared to each time: _____, _____, _____, _____, and _____.

QUESTIONS FOR DEEPER CONSIDERATION AND DISCUSSION

1. Consider the 5 events listed for the 3 months of persecution. Think of how each event might have increased the anger of Jesus' enemies.

2. Other religions are often based on visions of individuals, with no other witnesses. How does the Bible differ from that when it comes to the resurrection of Jesus? Why does the focus on multiple appearances—and multiple witnesses living at the time the accounts were written—build credibility?

LIFE OF JESUS	
Periods	**Events**
30 Years—Preparation	Birth Flight Return Baptism Temptation
First Year—Obscurity	First Miracle First Cleansing of the Temple Nicodemus Woman of Samaria Nobleman's Son
Second Year—Popularity	Calling Fishermen Sermon on the Mount Widow's Son Lakeside Parables Jairus's Daughter
Third Year—Opposition	Feeding 5,000 Syrophoenician's Daughter Peter's Confession Transfiguration Good Samaritan
Last 3 Months—Persecution	Lazarus 10 Healed of Leprosy Little Children Rich Young Ruler Zaccheus
Last Week—Passion Week	Mary's Anointing Triumphal Entry 10 Virgins Upper Room Crucifixion
40 Days—Resurrection Appearances	Appearance to 2 Appearance to 10 Appearance to 7 Appearance to 500 Appearance to 11

Adapted from *Standard Bible Atlas*, © Standard Publishing.

THE APOSTLES AND THE GREAT COMMISSION

After rising from the dead, Jesus commissioned His apostles to give the whole world the good news of His victory and His offer of salvation.

——— THE APOSTLES ———
A. WHO WERE THE APOSTLES?

First, they were 12 disciples whom Jesus chose early in His ministry. They appear in different order in the 3 different lists (Matthew 10:2-4; Luke 6:13-16; Acts 1:13). Nevertheless, they seemed to always be in 3 groups of 4:
- Simon Peter and Andrew, James and John
- Philip and Bartholomew, Thomas and Matthew
- James (the son of Alpheus) and Thaddeus, Simon (the Zealot) and Judas Iscariot

Note that 2 of them were named Simon: Simon Peter and Simon the Zealot (or Canaanite). And 2 were named James: James (along with his brother John) was a fisherman and the son of Zebedee, and James the son of Alpheus. Mark calls this second James "the less" (or "the younger," Mark 15:40), probably because he was younger or shorter than the other James. There were also 2 apostles named Judas: the infamous Judas Iscariot, and Thaddeus is sometimes called Judas son of James.

There are some understandable reasons why a man may have 2 names, or even 3. One reason is that the native language of the apostles (Aramaic) was different from the common language of the Roman Empire (Greek). So just like someone named Ian by a Scottish family may be called John in America or someone with the given name Jose might be called Joe by English-speaking friends, the apostles were referred to by names that meant the same thing in different languages.

This close group also used nicknames. Judas son of James must have been known for having a big heart, since his nicknames in 2 different languages (Thaddeus and Lebbeus) meant that. Jesus gave Simon the nickname of Peter, or Cephas, meaning "rock" (John 1:42). Perhaps Matthew the tax collector (also called Levi) once thought of himself as "God's gift" (as we would joke of a vain person today), because that is exactly what the name Matthew means! We know 1 famous apostle only by a nickname, Thomas. Perhaps he had a twin or was seen as someone quick to agree and so was called Twin, or Ditto. That is the translation of both Thomas and another name sometimes used, Didymus (John 11:16). The disciples may be referred to by a family name. Peter is sometimes described as Bar-jona, which means "son of John," and Bartholomew (who is sometimes called Nathanael, John 1:45) means "son of Tolmai."

Judas Iscariot hanged himself after betraying Christ; therefore, his name doesn't appear in the list of apostles in Acts 1. After Jesus ascended to Heaven, the disciples, seeking divine help in their choice, named Matthias to take Judas's place (Acts 1:15-26). Later Jesus chose Paul to be an apostle to the Gentiles (26:15-18).

B. WHAT WERE THE APOSTLES?

The word *apostle* means "someone sent out." Jesus gave that name to 12 of His disciples because He sent them to be the leaders in carrying His message to the world. The apostles were eyewitnesses. They saw Jesus after He rose from the dead. From their own personal knowledge, they could testify to His resurrection.

The apostles were also inspired. In a special way the Holy Spirit guided them into all truth and helped them remember what Jesus had taught them (John 14:26; 16:13). Infallibly, therefore, the apostles' teaching was Jesus' teaching. In a similar way, the apostles had miraculous powers as evidence of the presence and power of the Holy Spirit.

——— THE GREAT COMMISSION ———

Jesus gave the Great Commission several times and in different ways: Matthew 28:19, 20; Mark 16:15, 16; Acts 1:8. Memorize Matthew 28:19, 20.

While this commission was given specifically to the apostles, the other early Christians helped to carry it out; and every Christian today is expected to do his part. But since Christians today are not inspired as the apostles were, every Christian must be careful to teach just what the inspired apostles taught.

MAIN IDEAS OF THIS LESSON

The word *apostle* means "someone _____ out."

An important qualification of the apostles is that they were _____, allowing them to clearly testify to what they had seen.

Because they were specially gifted by the Holy Spirit, the apostles' testimony was without _____. That testimony was certified as true because of their ability to perform authenticating _____.

QUESTIONS FOR DEEPER CONSIDERATION AND DISCUSSION

1. Imagine that a friend is confused because some of the apostles are referred to by more than 1 name. How would you explain why that fact actually shows the Bible's accuracy, not its inaccuracy?

2. Paraphrase the Great Commission Jesus gave to His apostles. What are some ways we may also fulfill that commission?

BEGINNINGS OF THE CHURCH

—— THE BEGINNING IN —— JERUSALEM

A. THE FIRST DAY

The church began its work on the Day of Pentecost, 50 days after Jesus rose from the dead and 10 days after He ascended to Heaven. Following His instructions, the apostles were waiting in Jerusalem. Jews from many nations gathered there to celebrate the feast of Pentecost, 1 of the 3 great festivals. By our modern method of counting time, it was probably early in June, AD 30. Two important events of that day are worth noting:

1. *The coming of the Holy Spirit*—With a sound like a great wind and an appearance like tongues of fire, the Holy Spirit came to the apostles. He guided their thoughts as Jesus had promised (John 16:13, 14). He also enabled the apostles to speak in foreign languages so that Jews from many countries could understand the message (Acts 2:1-11).

2. *The message and the results*—Peter's sermon cited Old Testament prophecies to show that the Christ could not be held by death. Then he gave the testimony of the apostles that Jesus had risen. On this basis he declared that Jesus was the Christ. Many of the hearers had consented to the crucifixion of Jesus a few weeks before. Conscience-stricken, they asked what they should do. Peter urged them to repent and be baptized, and he promised the gift of the Holy Spirit (Acts 2:38). Three thousand people responded and were baptized.

B. THE EARLY CHURCH IN JERUSALEM

As the apostles continued to preach the same message, other thousands responded. The number of men reached 5,000 (Acts 4:4), and then even more multitudes were added (5:14). Even many of the priests became followers of Jesus (6:7), possibly some of the very Pharisees with whom Jesus had argued while on earth!

Led by the apostles, the church in Jerusalem instituted practices that fit their situation. Following Jesus would lead to persecution, which could mean separation from the support of families and the local synagogue. In response, believers acknowledged that their possessions belonged to their brothers and sisters as much as to them. Many sold property in order to care for the needy (Acts 2:44, 45; 4:32-37). Private property continued to be held, but gifts were made voluntarily. There is no biblical evidence that this same communal living pattern in Jerusalem was found in any other congregation.

When conflicts arose (as they always do when *people* are involved!), steps were taken to correct them. When there were questions about the fairness of how gifts were distributed to the needy, the apostles had the church choose 7 men to handle that job. These 7 are often called the first deacons, though the Bible does not give them that name. Among them were Stephen and Philip (not the apostle Philip), who became noted evangelists.

As Jesus foretold, those who had crucified Him soon began to persecute the apostles who declared He had risen. Acts 4 records an example. Imprisonment and beatings were frequent, and it is thought that all the apostles except John finally died for their faith. Especially bitter was the opposition aroused by Stephen's vigorous teaching. Finding his arguments too much for them, his opponents finally resorted to violence and stoned him to death. He was the first follower of Jesus to die for the faith (Acts 6:8–7:60).

——— BEGINNINGS IN JUDEA ——— AND SAMARIA

With the stoning of Stephen, persecution became so violent that the disciples scattered from Jerusalem to save their lives. But wherever they went, they took the story of Jesus and won others to Him (Acts 8:1-4).

Philip was an effective evangelist in Samaria (Acts 8:4-13). Then an angel sent him to meet and convert an Ethiopian on the way to Gaza (vv. 26-39). Afterward he preached in Azotus and other cities as he went to Caesarea (v. 40).

With John, Peter toured Samaria with the gospel (Acts 8:14-25). Afterward he preached at various points in Judea. At Lydda he brought healing to Aeneas; at Joppa he raised Tabitha from the dead (9:32-43).

——— BEGINNINGS AMONG ——— THE GENTILES

At first the gospel was preached only to Jews and to Samaritans, who were partly Jewish by race and by faith. But Jesus intended His message for the whole world. By special revelation, God sent Peter to Caesarea to give the gospel to Cornelius, a devout Roman officer (Acts 10). Cornelius probably was the first Gentile follower of Christ.

In the city of Antioch, 300 miles north of Jerusalem, disciples preached freely to Gentiles. A great church grew up there, which included both Jews and Gentiles. There the disciples were first called Christians (Acts 11:19-26).

Very important to the growth of the church among Gentiles was the conversion of Saul, later known as Paul (Acts 9:1-20). Saul approved the execution of Stephen. After that, he actively arrested and imprisoned believers. But Jesus confronted Saul while he was traveling to continue this persecution. Though Saul was a Jew, Jesus chose him to be a special apostle to Gentiles.

MAIN IDEAS OF THIS LESSON

The church began in the city of _____ on the Day of _____.

The first Christian to give his life for his faith was _____. That execution resulted in a great _____ of the church in Jerusalem.

Persecution drove Christians from Jerusalem, resulting in 2 non-Jewish groups of people entering the church—_____ (Jews who had intermarried with their Assyrian captors) and _____ (the first of which was an army officer named Cornelius).

1. Describe the early social arrangement of the church in Jerusalem and why it probably came about. In what ways are we expected to follow that example today?

2. While God does not cause suffering, God can use suffering for His purposes. Describe how the execution of Stephen helped bring about the expansion of the church.

CONVERSIONS IN THE BOOK OF ACTS	
Acts 2:1-8, 36-42	3,000 are baptized on Pentecost.
Acts 2:43-47	The Lord "added to the church daily" (v. 47).
Acts 4	Many who heard the word believed. And the number of the men was about 5,000 (v. 4).
Acts 8:1-17	Philip preaches in Samaria, where many believe and are baptized.
Acts 8:26-38	Philip teaches an Ethiopian, who believes and is baptized.
Acts 9:3-18; 22:6-16	Saul of Tarsus is converted and is baptized.
Acts 10	Peter teaches Cornelius and his household, and they are all baptized.
Acts 16:13-15	Lydia and her family are baptized.
Acts 16:25-34	The Philippian jailer and his household believe and are baptized.
Acts 18:8	Crispus, the chief ruler of the synagogue, believed on the Lord with all his house; and many of the Corinthians hearing believed, and were baptized.
Acts 18:24-28	Priscilla and Aquila teach Apollos the way of God more perfectly (v. 26).
Acts 19:1-7	Paul baptizes 12 disciples who previously knew only John's baptism.

Adapted from *Standard Bible Atlas,* © Standard Publishing.

NEW LIFE IN CHRIST

—— A NEW CREATURE ——

The apostle Paul wrote that becoming a Christian is more than adopting a new philosophy. When a person becomes a Christian, all phases of life are new (2 Corinthians 5:17).

A. A NEW STANDARD

God became flesh, and now we can see how He intends for us to live. We try to be, and lead others to be, not only Christian but Christlike. We ask, "What would Jesus do?"

B. A NEW HOPE

People may equate hope with wishful thinking. But real hope is based on the authority of whoever is offering it. God has promised forgiveness of sins, strength to overcome temptation, and eternal life to the faithful. We cannot create or earn any of these for ourselves, but we can trust in God to supply them.

C. A NEW OUTLOOK

People take measures to postpone death. But even if we have excellent health and everything the world can give, life cannot reach beyond the grave. Because death is conquered in Christ, we can focus on giving our lives away for the good of others now.

D. A NEW INCENTIVE

Disappointments and disillusionment come to all. When everything seems to go wrong, those involved may say, "What's the use?" But to the Christian, a disappointment is only a delay of blessings hoped for. Even when the world has done its worst, we have an incentive to go on, for our greatest hope lies beyond this world.

E. A NEW PURPOSE

When people view life as the sum of their possessions, they can easily become selfish. Yet Christians know it is more blessed to give than to receive. Our purpose is to serve and please Him who loved us enough to die for us.

F. A NEW REWARD

The world may offer riches, fame, power, learning, social achievement, and other desirable things; but it cannot offer what God offers to those in Christ—a forgiven life, a transformed life, eternal life, victory over sin and death, and a home in Heaven.

G. NEW DUTIES

We are saved to serve—not to serve ourselves but to serve others. We imitate Him who came as a servant king (Mark 10:45). Gathering with other believers, helping the needy in the name of Christ, and giving the gospel to others are some of the duties of a Christian.

H. New obligations

In Christ we have become children of God. We owe our Father reverence, loyalty, service, and love. But these obligations are a joy rather than a burden, an opportunity rather than a hardship.

I. New behavior

Wrongdoing of any kind is incompatible with our new life in Christ. We always try to do what is pleasing to the Master who has given us life. Purity, honesty, justice, unselfishness, charity, love, and service take on new importance.

—— NEW LIFE AND CHRISTIAN —— ORDINANCES

The Christian ordinances of baptism and the Lord's Supper are vitally related to new life in Christ. As mentioned in lesson 15, these ordinances, like the Jewish feasts of the Old Testament, are participatory acts that celebrate God's work in our lives.

A. Baptism

Authority for baptism—In speaking of ordinances of the church, we mean that Christ *ordered* the church to observe them. Throughout history, the church has been given freedom to use practices that work in their situations (such as building meeting places, using differing worship styles, etc.). But the ordinances of baptism and the Lord's Supper are different. Christ himself commanded them to be performed throughout the age. We find authority for baptism in Matthew 28:18-20; Mark 16:15, 16; and Acts 2:38.

Meaning of baptism—In baptism, a believer publicly associates with Jesus' death, burial, and resurrection by being "buried" in and then "resurrected" from the water (Romans 6:1-14). A past life of sin is buried, and a new life of doing right—empowered by the Holy Spirit—is beginning.

B. The Lord's Supper

Authority for the Lord's Supper—As is the case with baptism, Jesus instituted the Lord's Supper. He said, "This do in remembrance of me." We find the origin of this ordinance in Matthew 26:26-28; Mark 14:22-25; Luke 22:15-20; and 1 Corinthians 11:23-26.

Meaning of the Lord's Supper—The Lord's Supper has both a "vertical" and "horizontal" dimension. When the church participates in this practice, we *look up*, affirming our conviction that Jesus sacrificed His own body and shed His own blood for us. As a community we place ourselves at the same table as the first apostles and renew our determination to give ourselves wholly to Him. But we also *look around* to those participating with us. Because we all are partaking of the same "flesh and blood" of the elements, we recognize that the church is the body of Christ. Not only are we renewing our "vertical" allegiance to Christ; we are also affirming our "horizontal" allegiance to our brothers and sisters in Christ. This is a matter of the utmost importance (1 Corinthians 11:29; 12:27).

In baptism, a new believer publicly associates with the
_____, _____, and
_____ of Jesus.

In the Lord's Supper, the church remembers that Jesus _____
His own body and _____ His own blood for us. We
also recognize that the church is the _____ of
_____, and we renew our commitment to each other.

QUESTIONS FOR DEEPER CONSIDERATION AND DISCUSSION

1. Review the 9 implications of being a new creation in Jesus that are discussed in this lesson. Choose 2 or 3 and tell why they are especially meaningful to you. What might you add to this list?

2. Exactly how the 2 ordinances of the church should be kept has stirred controversy among professing believers over the centuries. Of what controversies are you aware? How do you believe those controversies can be resolved?

DATE	EVENTS IN PAUL'S LIFE—PART I
c. 5 BC	Saul (Paul) born in Tarsus, capital of the province of Cilicia (in modern-day Turkey)
c. AD 25–35	Saul educated and rises to prominence as a Pharisee
c. AD 32–35	Stephen executed
c. AD 32–35	Saul persecutes the church
c. AD 35	Saul of Tarsus meets Jesus on the way to Damascus
c. AD 35	Saul meets Ananias at the house of Judas
c. AD 35	Saul goes to Arabia
c. AD 38	Saul returns to Damascus
c. AD 38	Saul visits Jerusalem and church leaders
c. AD 38	Saul returns to Tarsus
c. AD 45	Barnabas seeks Saul to work with him in Antioch

LIFE OF PAUL—PART 1

In the recorded history of the early church, no one is more prominent than the apostle Paul. In the book of Acts, 16 of the 28 chapters are devoted mainly to his work. Of 21 letters in the New Testament, 13 or 14 are his. We cannot say he did more than all the other apostles, but we know more *about* what he did.

This great apostle is called Saul earlier in the book of Acts and called Paul later in the book. As was the case with Jesus' disciples, Paul was a Hebrew in a Greek world. He probably used both names throughout his life, depending on whether he was in a Jewish or Greek environment. The use of the Greek name in Acts begins when he enters the Greek world on his first missionary journey (Acts 13:9).

For our study, the life of Paul is divided into 6 periods:
- Saul the student
- Saul the persecutor
- Saul the convert
- Paul the missionary
- Paul the author
- Paul the martyr

Three of these periods will be considered in this lesson.

—— SAUL THE STUDENT ——

A. THE STUDENT IN TARSUS

Saul was born in Tarsus, a city of Asia Minor. It was a Jewish custom to teach every boy a trade, and Saul became a tentmaker. Later he often supported himself by that trade while carrying on his evangelistic work. No doubt he was taught the Old Testament Scriptures both at home and in the synagogue. Even at this early age and in a heathen city, he may have been taught the strict ways of the Pharisees (Acts 23:6).

B. THE STUDENT IN JERUSALEM

For advanced study Saul went to Jerusalem, perhaps in his early teens. There he studied under Gamaliel (Acts 22:3), a recognized teacher and a member of the supreme council of the Jews. It was Gamaliel who later moved the council to save the lives of the apostles (5:33-40).

—— SAUL THE PERSECUTOR ——

Gamaliel's tolerant view of the apostles' work was not reflected in his student Saul. Being exceedingly zealous for the Jewish faith, Saul became a most fanatical persecutor.

A. The stoning of Stephen

Saul did not himself throw stones at Stephen, but he gave hearty consent and held the robes of his companions while they stoned Stephen to death (Acts 7:57–8:1). This may indicate that Saul held a position of authority in the synagogue.

B. Persecution in Jerusalem

After the death of Stephen, Saul took a furious part in arresting disciples in Jerusalem (Acts 8:3). He later said this persecution was "beyond measure" (Galatians 1:13) and a very great sin (see 1 Timothy 1:12-15).

C. The trip to Damascus

Not content to persecute disciples in Jerusalem, Saul asked the priests to authorize him to arrest Jewish disciples in foreign cities. He was sent to Damascus to seek out followers of Jesus and bring them back in chains (Acts 9:1, 2).

—— SAUL THE CONVERT ——

A. On the way to Damascus

Before he reached Damascus, Saul had a miraculous experience. The resurrected Christ appeared to him, convincing him that he was opposing the very Messiah whom he and all the Jews expected (Acts 9:1-8). Later Paul explained that Jesus appeared thus to make him a witness and an apostle (26:12-18).

B. In Damascus

Blinded by the brilliant vision of Jesus, Saul remained blind in Damascus for 3 days. Then the Lord sent a disciple named Ananias to restore his sight. Ananias then said, "Arise, and be baptized, and wash away thy sins, calling on the name of the Lord" (Acts 9:8-18; 22:11-16).

C. Saul as a new Christian

Saul spent 2 or 3 years in Arabia and Damascus. He left the city for a time, perhaps to find a quiet place where he could pray for guidance and restudy the Old Testament in light of the truth he had learned about Christ. But whenever he had the opportunity, he now proclaimed the gospel he had opposed—proclaimed it so forcefully that the Jews determined to kill him. They enlisted the help of the governor of Damascus, but Saul escaped and returned to Jerusalem. There he was hated by his former companions and feared by the disciples he once had sought to arrest and injure. The former persecutor now was bitterly persecuted.

D. Saul the fugitive

Thanks to kindly Barnabas, the disciples at Jerusalem finally accepted Saul. But the Jews plotted to kill him, so he fled back home to Tarsus. From there Barnabas summoned him to help in the rapidly growing church in Antioch. It was Antioch that became the base for Paul's famous missionary journeys.

We can study Paul's life by labeling each period by the role he played during that time. Those roles were _____, _____,

_____, _____, _____, and

_____.

Saul had studied under a renowned teacher by the name of _____.
Saul's zeal for his Jewish faith led him to be involved in the execution of

_____ and to arrest other Christians. He became

a Christian when he met the resurrected Jesus while traveling to the city of

_____.

QUESTIONS FOR DEEPER CONSIDERATION AND DISCUSSION

1. While it is popular to call almost any religion a "religion of peace," religious zeal can have a dark side. Why do you think this is? How did zeal for the Jewish law drive Saul to act less than peaceably?

2. Barnabas was an influential person in the life of Paul. His given name was Joseph; Barnabas was a nickname. Using a Bible dictionary or other study tool, find the meaning of that name. Talk about some ways his actions toward Paul showed why he deserved that nickname.

DATE	EVENTS IN PAUL'S LIFE—PART 2
AD 47–49	Paul's first missionary journey
AD 52–54	Paul's second missionary journey
c. AD 52	Paul has a vision calling him to Macedonia
AD 54–58	Paul's third missionary journey
AD 58	Paul arrested in Jerusalem
AD 61	Paul sent to Rome to be tried before Caesar
AD 61–63	Paul under house arrest in Rome
AD 67–68	Paul's second imprisonment
AD 68	Paul executed by Nero

LIFE OF PAUL—PART 2

Review the 3 periods of Paul's life covered in lesson 24. This lesson continues with the final 3 periods.

—— PAUL THE MISSIONARY ——

For a year or more, Saul taught in Antioch, and from that city he began his 3 famous missionary journeys. After these, the book of Acts records his eventful trip to Rome. Little is known of his later work.

A. First missionary journey—AD 47–49

Paul began his missionary work on the great island of Cyprus, not far from Antioch (of Syria). There he converted the Roman governor Sergius Paulus. From that time Saul was called Paul. From Cyprus he sailed north to the mainland. Moving inland through the mountains, he came to a city called by the same name as his starting point, Antioch (of Pisidia). From there he went on to Iconium, Lystra, and Derbe. Then he turned back and visited each of those places again, giving additional teaching to the new Christians before he returned to his starting point. Read the record in Acts 13, 14. Barnabas was Paul's companion on this journey; and on the first part of it, John Mark (who later wrote the Gospel of Mark) accompanied them.

B. Second missionary journey— AD 52–54

On the second tour Paul did not go to Cyprus, but traveled by land to visit the mainland churches he had started on the first trip. Then he went on west to Troas, from where he sailed across the narrow sea to Macedonia. At Philippi, Lydia was converted, then a jailer who had kept Paul in prison. Paul next preached in Thessalonica, then went on to Berea. Unbelieving Jews of Thessalonica opposed him bitterly in both places, and he went on to Athens, where he delivered his famous sermon on Mars' hill (the Areopagus). After that he worked a year and a half in Corinth, building a large church in a city noted for its sensuality and selfishness. From Corinth he turned eastward, stopping briefly at Ephesus and probably attending a Jewish feast at Jerusalem before returning to Antioch. Paul and Silas began this journey together. Timothy joined them at Lystra, and Luke was added to the party in Troas. This journey is recorded in Acts 15:36–18:22.

C. Third missionary journey—AD 54–58

On the third journey, Paul went from Antioch through the "upper coasts," or mountains, of Asia Minor (Acts 19:1), perhaps revisiting churches started on his first trip. Then he settled at Ephesus for about 3 years. Afterward he visited the churches in Macedonia and Greece, then sailed from Philippi by way of Troas and Miletus to Caesarea. From there he went on to Jerusalem to attend a Jewish feast. There a mob tried to kill him, but Roman soldiers stationed near the temple rescued him. The Roman governor returned him to Caesarea but kept him in prison for 2 years, AD 58–60. On the latter part of this trip, Luke was with Paul. Read the account in Acts 18:23–21:25.

D. THE TRIP TO ROME—AD 61

Seeing no hope of justice in Caesarea, Paul appealed to the Roman emperor. The governor then sent him to Rome for judgment. After a stormy voyage, the ship was wrecked on the island of Melita, or Malta as it is now called. The passengers spent the rest of the winter there and then took another ship to Puteoli, from which they proceeded to Rome on foot. Paul was a prisoner in Rome for 2 years, AD 61–63, and at that point the book of Acts ends. Luke was with Paul on this eventful trip. See the record in Acts 27:1–28:16.

E. LATER TRAVELS—AD 63–68

The book of Acts ends with Paul a prisoner in Rome. But in the letters to Timothy and Titus, there are hints that lead many scholars to think he was released and resumed his travels, revisiting churches in Asia and Macedonia, as well as teaching on the island of Crete. Old tradition indicates that he also went to Spain.

——— PAUL THE AUTHOR ———

Paul wrote about half the books of the New Testament—13 or 14. Some were written during busy missionary tours, others while he was a prisoner in Rome. This, therefore, is not really another period but another activity of his missionary period.

Some of his letters, such as Romans and Thessalonians, were written to churches. Others were written to individuals, such as Timothy, Titus, and Philemon.

——— PAUL THE MARTYR ———

In AD 64, the Roman emperor Nero launched a great persecution against the Christians, whom he accused of starting a disastrous fire in Rome. The persecution continued about 4 years. Tradition has it that Paul was arrested and put to death near the end of this time.

——— OTHER APOSTOLIC WORK ———

The Bible gives no information about the ministries of most of the apostles. Nevertheless, tradition tells stories of their missionary work all over the known world. Also, because of the writings of Peter and John, we do know a little of their later work.

Peter fled Jerusalem after his escape from prison (Acts 12). We know of a controversial visit by Peter to the church in Antioch, during which Paul accused him of hypocrisy (Galatians 2:11-14). Possibly when Paul was in prison, Peter wrote words of encouragement to Christians in many of the Gentile churches Paul founded (1 Peter 1:1). At the end of Peter's letters, he seems to give Paul's letters authority equivalent to that of Old Testament Scripture (2 Peter 3:14-16).

John is probably the only apostle who lived and worked for a long time after Paul died. Early Christian writings outside the Bible indicate that he lived in Ephesus after Jerusalem was destroyed in AD 70. Between AD 70 and 100, John wrote his Gospel, 3 letters, and Revelation. Many evangelical scholars date all these between AD 90 and 100.

MAIN IDEAS OF THIS LESSON

Between the years of AD 47 and 58, Paul took 3 _____ journeys. In his first he planted churches in Galatia and surrounding areas. In his second he went as far as modern-day Greece, spending a year and a half in the sensual and selfish city of _____. Three years of his third journey were spent in the second largest city of the Roman Empire of his day, _____.

We know some things about the later ministries of the apostles _____ and _____ because of their writings.

QUESTIONS FOR DEEPER CONSIDERATION AND DISCUSSION

1. Paul did not begin the church in Rome, but wanted to visit this largest city of the Roman Empire (Romans 1:8-13). He certainly had made some plans to go there. Consider the old saying, "Life is just what happens to you while you're busy making other plans." How does that saying apply to how Paul *actually* got to visit Rome?

2. Christians should not be contentious, but we should never be afraid to stand up for what we know is right. Using concordances, trace the rocky relationships between Paul and Peter and between Paul and John Mark. How did the conflicts end up being resolved?

THE APOSTLES AND CHRISTIAN TRADITION

While the Bible does not tell us where most of the apostles brought the gospel, early Christian traditions provides some answers.

Apostles	Where tradition says they traveled
Andrew	Russia, Asia Minor, Greece
Thomas	India
Philip	North Africa, Asia Minor
Matthew	Persia, Ethiopia
Bartholomew	India, Armenia, Ethiopia, southern Arabia
James (the son of Alpheus)	Syria
Simon (the Zealot)	Persia

THE BIBLE FOR THE WHOLE WORLD

—— THE DIVINE PURPOSE ——

A. GOD'S WANTS TO BLESS THE WORLD

God chose Abraham for that purpose (Genesis 22:17, 18). Because He loved the whole world, He sent His Son to redeem it (John 3:16). The redeemed of all nations shall share His eternal home (Revelation 21:23-27).

B. JESUS SENDS US TO TEACH THE WORLD

The gospel is for every creature (Mark 16:15, 16). Every teaching of Christ is for all nations (Matthew 28:19, 20).

—— MISSIONARY EXAMPLES ——

A. CHRIST HIMSELF WAS A MISSIONARY

The word *missionary* comes from a Latin word that means "send." Christ was sent to reveal God's will as well as to redeem, and He sends His people in like manner (John 20:21). His people should imitate Him in their devotion to doing God's will and to making it known.

B. PAUL WAS A MISSIONARY

Paul wrote about half the books of the New Testament. This is some indication of the extent of his missionary work, for he wrote mostly to people and churches involved in that work.

C. THE FIRST CHRISTIANS WERE MISSIONARIES

Scattered from Jerusalem, they went everywhere preaching the word (Acts 8:4). Examples of Christian teachers are Ananias of Damascus (22:10-16) and Aquila and Priscilla (18:24-26).

D. THE CHURCH HAS A MESSAGE

The Gospels tell the story of Christ's own mission in the world. Acts tells of the missionary work of the church. Many letters were written by missionaries to their mission fields. Revelation 22:17 urges those who respond to God's call to extend that call to others.

—— THE NEED OF THE WORLD ——

A. THE WORLD NEEDS GOD'S WORD

Though nature is a partial revelation of God, people without His Word drift farther and farther from Him (Romans 1:18-25; Proverbs 29:18). All have sinned, and the wages of sin is death (Romans 3:23; 6:23).

B. THE GOSPEL SAVES

Romans 1:16 says that the gospel "is the power of God unto salvation." If God's people had not brought the gospel to us or to our ancestors in bygone years, we could have no hope of salvation. If we do not continue to take the gospel to others, countless millions will be lost.

—— THE WORD AND —— THE WORLD TODAY

A. WHAT HAS BEEN ACCOMPLISHED

There is hardly a country in the world where the gospel has not been heard by some. Thousands of missionaries are constantly at work to reach others. Parts of the Bible have been translated into more than 2,000 languages.

B. WHAT REMAINS TO BE DONE

Probably two-thirds of the world's people are not Christian. Many isolated tribal people have been touched but slightly by Christian teaching and do not have a translation of the Bible in their native languages. A new start is possible in populous countries where Communist governments have bitterly opposed Christianity. In all lands, most Christians have neighbors who are not Christians. There is work to be done next door as well as around the world.

MAIN IDEAS OF THIS LESSON

God's purpose to _____ the whole world can be accomplished if we fulfill our commission to _____ the whole world.

The teaching of Christ is for all _____. This can be seen because Jesus himself, Paul, and the early Christians could be described as

_____.

QUESTIONS FOR DEEPER CONSIDERATION AND DISCUSSION

1. A popular view is that Christians are intolerant for believing that we should try to persuade people of different cultures to accept Christianity rather than remain with their cultural religions. How would you respond to that charge?

2. Consider the challenges that remain in taking the gospel to the world. List some steps you can take personally to address 1 or 2 of these challenges.

THE MEANING OF THE BOOK OF REVELATION

As mentioned earlier on pages 20 and 21, not all Bible-believing Christians agree about how to interpret the last book of the Bible.

Here are some big ideas from Revelation, however, that are universally held by believers.

Jesus remains present with his church. The book of Revelation is filled with vivid word pictures. Individual churches are described as lamps, sending the light of Jesus' message to the world. Jesus is pictured as one who walks among those lamps, tending the flames. Even in the darkest times, the church has light and Jesus is present to keep it lit!

Satan uses human leaders to harass the church. The ancient serpent who deceived Adam and Eve in the beginning will be around until the end. John pictures Satan as a great dragon bent on destroying the church. In John's vision, the dragon empowers an ugly beast wearing royal crowns to persecute the church. But the fate of this beast is certain. Human leaders may harass the church, but they will be destroyed.

The inheritance of Adam and Eve will be ours again. When Adam and Eve rebelled against God, they were evicted from their perfect home. But because Jesus paid the price of that rebellion, the descendants of Adam and Eve will again have access to paradise. The tree of life, once in the middle of Eden, will have a prominent place in the New Jerusalem John described.

Excerpt from *Discovering God's Story,* © Standard Publishing.

PRONUNCIATION GUIDE

ABEDNEGO. Uh-*bed*-nee-go

ARMAGEDDON. Are-muh-*ged*-un

BAAL. *Bay*-ul

BABYLONIANS. Bab-ih-*low*-nee-unz

BARTHOLOMEW. Bar-*thahl*-uh-mew

BELSHAZZAR. Bel-*shazz*-er

CAESAR AUGUSTUS. *See*-zer Aw-*gus*-tus

CAESAREA. Sess-uh-*ree*-uh

CAIAPHAS. *Kay*-uh-fus or *Kye*-uh-fus

CAPERNAUM. Kuh-*per*-nay-um

CEPHAS. *See*-fus

CHINNERETH. *Kin*-eh-reth or *Chin*-neh-reth

CORNELIUS. Cor-*neel*-yus

DECAPOLIS. Dee-*cap*-uh-lis

DIDYMUS. *Did*-uh-mus

DOMITIAN. Duh-*mish*-un

EMMANUEL. E-*man*-you-el

EMMAUS. Em-*may*-us

EPHRAIM. *Ee*-fray-im

EZEKIEL. Ee-*zeek*-ee-ul or Ee-*zeek*-yul

FRANKINCENSE. *frank*-in-sense

GALATIANS. Guh-*lay*-shunz

GAMALIEL. Guh-*may*-lih-ul or Guh-*may*-lee-al

GENTILES. *Jen*-tiles

GETHSEMANE. Geth-*sem*-uh-nee

GOLGOTHA. *Gahl*-guh-thuh

GOMORRAH. Guh-*more*-uh

HABAKKUK. Huh-*back*-kuk

HAGGAI. *Hag*-eye or *Hag*-ay-eye

IMMANUEL. Ih-*man*-you-el

ISHMAEL. *Ish*-may-el

ISSACHAR. *Izz*-uh-kar

JAPHETH. *Jay*-feth

JEHOSHAPHAT. Jeh-*hosh*-uh-fat

LEVITES. *Lee*-vites

LEVITICUS. Leh-*vit*-ih-kus

MACCABEES. *Mack*-uh-bees

MACEDONIA. Mass-eh-*doe*-nee-uh

MELCHIZEDEK. Mel-*kiz*-eh-dek

MESSIAH. Meh-*sigh*-uh

MESSIANIC. mess-ee-*an*-ick

MOSAIC. Mo-*zay*-ik

MOSES. *Mo*-zes or *Mo*-zez

NAPHTALI. *Naf*-tuh-lye

NEBUCHADNEZZAR. *Neb*-yuh-kud-**nez**-er

OBADIAH. O-buh-*dye*-uh

PATRIARCHS. *pay*-tree-arks

PENTATEUCH. *Pen*-ta-teuk

PENTECOST. *Pent*-ih-kost

PHARISEES. *Fair*-ih-seez

PHILEMON. Fih-*lee*-mun or Fye-*lee*-mun

PONTIUS PILATE. *Pon*-shus or *Pon*-ti-us *Pie*-lut

SADDUCEES. *Sad*-you-seez

SAMARITANS. Suh-*mare*-uh-tunz

SEPTUAGINT. Sep-*too*-ih-jent

SOLOMON. *Sol*-o-mun

SYNAGOGUE. *sin*-uh-gog

SYROPHOENICIAN. *Sigh*-roe-fih-**nish**-un

TABERNACLE. **tah**-ber-*na*-kul

UZZIAH. Uh-*zye*-uh

ZACCHEUS. Zack-*key*-us

ZECHARIAH. *Zek*-uh-**rye**-uh

ZEPHANIAH. Zef-uh-*nye*-uh

Adapted from *Standard Bible Dictionary*, © Standard Publishing.

───── SELECTED BIBLIOGRAPHY ─────

Benware, Paul. *Survey of the New Testament—Bible Commentary.* Chicago: Moody Publishers, 2004.

———. *Survey of the Old Testament—Bible Commentary.* Chicago: Moody Publishers, revised edition, 2001.

Christianity Today International, JoHannah Reardon, editor. *Crash Course on the Old Testament.* Cincinnati: Standard Publishing, 2008.

———, Brad Lewis, editor. *Crash Course on the New Testament.* Cincinnati: Standard Publishing, 2008.

Draper, Charles W. and Chad Brand and Archie England, editors. *Holman Illustrated Bible Dictionary.* Nashville: Holman Reference, revised edition, 2003.

Eichenberger, Jim. *Discovering God's Story.* Cincinnati: Standard Publishing, 2010.

Halley, Henry H. *Halley's Bible Handbook.* Grand Rapids, MI: Zondervan, 1965 edition.

Hendriksen, William. *Survey of the Bible: A Treasury of Bible Information.* Ada, MI: Baker Books, 4th edition, 1995.

New Testament Maps and Charts. Cincinnati: Standard Publishing, 2000.

Old Testament Maps and Charts. Cincinnati: Standard Publishing, 2000.

Rasmussen, Carl G. *Zondervan Atlas of the Bible.* Grand Rapids, MI: Zondervan, 2010.

Rhodes, Ron. *The Complete Guide to Bible Translations.* Eugene, OR: Harvest House Publishers, 2009.

Rose Book of Bible Charts, Maps, and Time Lines. Torrance, CA: Rose Publishing, Inc., spiral-bound, 2005.

Sailhamer, John H. *The Books of the Bible.* Grand Rapids, MI: Zondervan, 1998.

———. *How We Got the Bible.* Grand Rapids, MI: Zondervan, 1998.

Standard Bible Atlas. Cincinnati: Standard Publishing, 2008 edition.

Standard Bible Dictionary. Cincinnati: Standard Publishing, 2006.

Standard Reference Library. Cincinnati: Standard Publishing—

- Old Testament Volume 1: *The Pentateuch.* Compiled by Douglas Redford, 2008.

- Old Testament Volume 2: *The History of Israel.* Compiled by Douglas Redford, 2008.

- Old Testament Volume 3: *Poetry and Prophecy.* Compiled by Larry Pechawer, 2008.

- New Testament Volume 1: *The Life and Ministry of Jesus.* Compiled by Douglas Redford, 2007.

- New Testament Volume 2: *The New Testament Church.* Compiled by Douglas Redford, 2007.

Stone, Larry. *The Story of the Bible.* Nashville: Thomas Nelson, 2010.

Strong, James. *The New Strong's Expanded Exhaustive Concordance of the Bible.* Nashville: Thomas Nelson, expanded edition, 2010.

Tenney, Merrill C. *New Testament Survey.* Grand Rapids, MI: Eerdmans Publishing Company, 1985.